MERLIN

GORDON THORBURN

MERLIN

The true story of a courageous police horse

JOHN BLAKE

Published by John Blake Publishing Ltd,
3 Bramber Court, 2 Bramber Road,
London W14 9PB, England

www.johnblakepublishing.co.uk

www.facebook.com/Johnblakepub **facebook**
twitter.com/johnblakepub **twitter**

First published in hardback in 2014

ISBN: 978-1-78219-465-1

British Library Cataloguing-in-Publication Data:
a catalogue record for this book is available from the British Library.

Design by www.envydesign.co.uk

Printed in Great Britain by CPI Group (UK) Ltd

1 3 5 7 9 10 8 6 4 2

Papers used b | :s made
from wood gro | conform
to th |

Every atten | lders,
but some wer | e people

'The great point in teaching a horse is to know, when he refuses to obey, whether he does so from caprice, obstinacy, vice, or from ignorance, and in this lies the only difficulty. If the horse does not understand what you want, and you punish him because he does not understand you, will he then understand you better?'

FRANÇOIS BAUCHER, *RIDING MASTER, 1842*

'The instructor should insist on the men using their horses gently; he will thus save much time, and gain his object.'

CAPTAIN LOUIS NOLAN, *15TH HUSSARS, 1852*

'We don't use carrot and stick, because we don't need the stick.'

JO SULLIVAN, *METROPOLITAN POLICE HORSE TRAINER, 2013*

Contents

Acknowledgements

This book could not have been written without the unstinting help of officers in the Metropolitan Police Mounted Branch and the trainers at Imber Court. My thanks go to them all, but I must mention especially trainer Jo Sullivan and Merlin's partner in crime, PC Karen Howell. Merlin himself has been the model of graciousness throughout, and has allowed the author to give him Polo mints. Other very welcome helpers and contributors (and horses) are mentioned as we go along, but I must finally mention PS Craig Richards for the use of the photo of him and Merlin on the back of the jacket, and Neil Paterson, of the MPS Heritage Centre manager, for help with historical photographs, as well as for his comprehensive knowledge of the Met's history.

The nine photographs on pages 2, 3 and 4, and the upper and lower-left photographs on page 5, of the plates section, credited in the captions as '*MPS*', were sourced from the Metropolitan Police Heritage Centre. The images are © copyright of the Commissioner of Police for the Metropolis.

The Metropolitan Police Heritage Centre, which is open to the public on weekdays (see website: http://www.metpolicehistory.co.uk/met-police-heritage-centre.html), is at The Annexe, Empress State Building, Empress Approach, Lillie Road, West Brompton, London SW6 1TR; telephone: 020-7161 1234.

Other photographs are credited in the captions.

Chapter One

Why Do We Have Merlins?

A hundred years and more ago, the world depended on horses. Police had them, cabbies had them, the grocer's boy drove one, omnibuses were pulled by them, well-to-do families went to town and church in their carriages and traps, farmers cultivated the land with horses, every wayside inn had stables, and soldiers went to war on them. But that was a long time gone. Horses now are just for the countryside, for leisure, and racing, of course. So why do the police want them?

Among the favourite topics of politicians and police commanders alike are: (1) cutting costs, and (2) police presence in the public eye. The neutral observer might argue that these two topics do not fit together very well, and that more of the former will surely result in less of the latter. Even so, where a police force must save money and it has a Mounted Branch, the horses, the most obvious form of police presence, are always put forward for potential budgetary execution. Perhaps, to the accountants, they look like an unquantifiable expense.

Horses must be fed and looked after. They're working the streets so they need to be shod regularly, and the vet's bills would make your eyes water. Mounted officers spend a considerable part of their time being stable lads and lasses on police pay. Talking of stables, that land and those buildings could be sold. And is all that training, for months and months, really necessary? Then again, these equine coppers have an easy time of it. The Chief Constable looks at the books and sees X number of extra beat bobbies for no extra money, if the Force were to get rid of the horses. Instead of doing proper police work, chasing villains and drunk drivers, these same potential foot- and motor-police go jolly jogging around on horseback as if they're on a holiday, don't they?

By 'police presence', politicians and senior officers mean a combination of image and visibility. No one could argue with the visibility of an officer on a horse, and very few would argue that the mounted officer is not good for the image. The public like the horses, and they feel cheered by the notion that this large, gentle, official creature is somehow on their side. A mounted officer breaks down barriers between the police and public; the horse attracts and engages people, who will come up to pet and talk to the animal – and the officer.

West Yorkshire Police tried an experiment. Two officers on foot were stationed at a point in the city centre busy with pedestrians. In two hours, they were approached with enquiries six times. When two mounted officers were stationed in the same place, they had so many questions and engagements with the public that they couldn't keep count.

'Nobody ever tried to pet my police car, but they line up to pet my horse.'

Police officer, Washington, DC

When it comes to police business, the horse–officer combination is authoritative, even intimidating, but without effort or aggression. The implication of an officer in complete charge of a very large and potentially dangerous animal is that he/she deserves respect, and the officer–horse team projects a feeling of stability and control.

A police helicopter can be seen as the spy in the sky by folk on the ground; the same people regard the officer and horse as 'one of us'. Put a dozen, two dozen, even 50 officers on foot between two opposing large groups of protesters who are trying to get at each other and the situation is in the balance, and the balance might tip the wrong way. Send in two or three mounted officers and the protesters will most likely back off, and the matter will be resolved without physical force.

The budget holders will still query whether there is value for money in a Mounted Unit, so much so that a research study has been commissioned to examine how Mounted Units in England and Wales help Forces deal with public order incidents and so on, and whether any cost-effectiveness measure can be placed against what they do all day. Researchers from Oxford University have gathered and analysed quantitative data on deployment, and are going on to observe Mounted sections over the course of a year.

Demonstrations can be good-natured, and even the largest can stay that way. Or, they may be potentially disruptive to everyone and everything around, sometimes fired up by those with their own causes. Or they can be openly hostile from the outset. Demos of course have a reason, and an object, against which the good-natured or hostile protest is directed. If the crowd begins to stray from the lawful to the unlawful, by intention or action, the police must step in, and hostility can easily transfer from the object of the demo to the police themselves, sometimes incurring serious violence and injury to horses and officers.

Prevention is much better than intervention, and extensive training has prepared the officer and his mount for all eventualities. From their high vantage points, mounted officers can spot potentially ugly confrontations, and bottlenecks where overcrowding and crushing may cause – as it almost certainly says on your insurance policy – riot and civil commotion. With their well-tried crowd management tactics, mounted officers can solve the problem before it gets out of hand. In such situations, one mounted officer can be as effective as 10 or more on foot, but the foot-police will be there too, often looking to the Mounted Branch to protect them from direct assault and/or to sort matters out so there will be no need for confrontation on foot.

The media are always present whenever there's a big demo. Of course, when choosing what to film and photograph, they don't bother when there's nothing happening, so when the Mounted Police are doing their job perfectly, and everybody's quiet and there's no disorder, no pictures result.

The police have to intervene when peace is threatened, or when minor disorder seems likely to become major. Usually, the intervention takes the form of arresting individuals who are turning up the tempo, or forming a blue line between factions, or stopping fights. In all these cases, the majority of the crowd will welcome police action, and the presence of officers on horseback will prove beneficial. To a certain extent, a happy result depends on how the crowd sees the police: as legitimate peacekeepers, or as a force on the side of one faction or another.

Essex Police horses Bella and Biscuit both needed stitches to wounds and were off work for a week after being bitten by a dog. Their riders, PC Frank Pallet and PC Sarah Fisk, were both thrown from their horses but were uninjured.

A 34-year-old local woman was arrested for having a dog dangerously out of control in a public place. A dog was seized and police investigated offences under Sections One and Three of the Dangerous Dogs Act (1991).

Bella needed stitches in two wounds to a shoulder and puncture wounds around her body. Biscuit was more seriously injured and had a deep cut to his near side foreleg and puncture wounds around his body. [Because of budget restrictions, the Essex Police Mounted Unit was disbanded in 2012.]

At football matches and other sporting events numbers can vary from the low thousands to the equivalent of a sizeable town's entire population. Once upon a time, ties took place at 3pm on Saturdays. Now, they can be at almost any hour on any day, perhaps with the away supporters, disgruntled at having lost, wanting to make a mark before they catch the last train home. Moods can very quickly swing from friendly banter to insults and discord, and this is when the restrained and disciplined presence and actions of the Mounted Police can be so invaluable.

At a Super Bowl game staged at Wembley Stadium, 10

mounted officers directed a crowd of 70,000. When thousands of fans invaded the pitch at a Bristol Rovers match, eight mounted officers cleared them off the grass in just two and a half minutes. There can be no doubt that if trouble does brew up between fans, mounted intervention is not only the most effective answer, it's the one preferred by all parties. The foot police don't want to get into hand-to-hand fighting, as can happen when they try to separate warring factions, and no one – including the clubs and the real fans, apart from the hooligans – wants the mayhem and injuries of a mass battle, nor do they wish to see it on the TV news.

A typical example of intervention occurred when a group of away supporters took over a pub and began offensive chants and songs, knowing the home supporters were going past on their way to the match. Unsurprisingly, some of the more assertive home fans also formed a group, and the group got bigger and bigger. mounted officers noticed and quickly placed themselves between the home fans and the pub. Problem solved.

The 'quickly' part of that little story is important. An officer on horseback can reach a trouble spot much faster than one on foot who may have to push his way through a solid queue of people.

An individual bent on bother, perhaps with his usual good nature and sensibilities suspended by excitement and beer, may feel that having a punch-up with a copper would be a good idea at the time, but he'd need to be extremely excited to pit his human strength against that of a very large horse. A ticket tout may feel free to operate in a dense, busy crowd but if he spots a mounted officer, he knows that he can see him, and catch up with him.

It is perhaps no surprise to common-sense folk that the likelihood of trouble, the number of arrests historically, the presence of Mounted Police and the size of the club are all factors that correlate fairly well. Arrests and Mounted Police go together when any of the big clubs, with their massive fan bases, are playing. The most 'serious' matches in London – the big derby games and those when the best-supported teams come to town – naturally attract the most planning time and the largest number of horses. There is a direct correlation between horse numbers and disorder: the more of the former, the less there is of the latter.

The approachability of Mounted Police, often attracting favourable comments when they are on normal duties, is another important factor at a football game. They're much more visible than foot officers, of course, but also far more likely to engage with the fans than police in protective kit, in cars or in surveillance positions. From the crowd's point of view also, the visibility and commanding presence of Mounted Police is reassuring for families and others who simply want to see the game and get home without having to dodge flying bottles.

Patrolling the streets and open spaces has been, and always will be, a major police priority. Law-abiding citizens want to see the police, and the minority with unlawful intent, don't. Officers on the beat and in patrol cars do a lot of the work but sometimes a pair of officers on horseback is the best option. Mounted officers can observe, smell and hear things that a patrol car crew can miss; people approach and tell them about things that they don't have a chance to tell officers in a car.

In recent times there has been a shift in the Met, from general, beat-bobby style walking around (called Safer

Neighbourhood Patrols) to more specifically tasked duties, often known as High Visibility. These directed patrols through particular areas are a deterrent where crime is known to be possible or even likely, especially the kind of low-level crime that affects the lives of ordinary, innocent people, such as theft – particularly from cars and shops – rowdiness and vandalism. These are the so-called 'signal crimes', the ones that have a general effect on local people out of proportion to their actual significance. Where there are many signal crimes committed, feelings of security and confidence in the Force go down, regardless of the incidence of major crime and police success against it.

In areas where confidence in the police is low, a gang of youths may well throw stones at a patrol car, and they may well see a mounted officer as a symbol of authority and repression, but they are far more likely to engage with horse and rider than the officer in the car.

These are what we might call the big issues, but there are highly specific and unusual situations where horse and officer can achieve success. One example was at a known suicide spot on the coast, where a regular patrol had a clear effect, which was credited to the sympathy and calm that seems to accompany the combination of large, kindly-looking animal and his understanding rider.

If only he'd had a horse, but an officer of the Royal Canadian Mounted Police was in a car when he was attacked by a bull moose. Heading towards a crossroads at Prince Rupert, British Columbia, trying to head off another vehicle coming that way, he saw two moose standing at the junction. One charged the car and jumped on the roof, smashing various bits of it and injuring the officer.

The two animals then ran off. The officer had a bruised shoulder, but finished his shift and went home to rest.

Street vendors in New York's Times Square wanted to report smoke rising from a car, believing it might be a bomb. Their first sight of authority was two Mounted Police who, on hearing about the smoke, were able to clear the Square before the Bomb Squad arrived.

Mounted officers are ideal for patrolling open spaces, where foot patrols would not be so effective. In the parks and byways, there can be criminal damage, anti-social behaviour, indecency or worse. Making these areas safe and trouble-free is what the local residents want, and the Mounted Branch is very good at it. The mounted officer can search and oversee far more than an officer on foot. There is an image dimension too. Surveys show that people remember mounted patrols better and so, even where the actual number of patrols may be no different, they feel that the policing of their area is more regular and thorough than when foot- and motor-patrols are deployed exclusively. In those areas of London that, as a rule, don't see mounted officers, public perception of police visibility is measurably lower than in those areas where they are seen. Whether this converts into greater trust and confidence is more difficult to measure, but it does seem reasonable to expect that it might. What cannot be doubted is the affection and admiration felt by the public towards their Mounted Police. In the United States, where civic offices are more often the subject of popular voting than in the UK, there have been several cases where the powers sought to close their Mounted Units for reasons of expense, only to have citizens express their disapproval so strongly that the threat had to be withdrawn.

Authority comes into it as well. Which symbol of authority is the strongest and most appealing: officer in car, officer on bicycle or officer on horseback? Is that at least partly because the (relatively small and weak) officer has obvious charge and control over the (relatively large and powerful) animal?

As with any police officer, members of the Mounted Branch can get the call to any kind of incident, across anything the human race has to offer, from traffic jams to fights, accidents to serious crime. Other branches of the police force will send for the cavalry when motorised and pedestrian police won't do, so that might be in a search-and-rescue operation or a suspect pursuit, over terrain where the horse and rider offer the best prospect of success. Land Rovers get stuck and run out of petrol; the Mounted team carry on no matter what the weather.

Where a mounted officer is on solo patrol and happens to be the first responder to a call and needs to arrest someone, or by chance comes across an incident requiring an arrest – or first aid, for that matter – there is an obvious difficulty. If the suspect needs to be restrained or subdued, the mounted officer must be sure that the horse will stand the while, not get excited, and not want to join in. Once matters are stable enough, the motorised infantry can take over, if need be.

This was not the case recently in Bristol, where an organised group of graffiti 'artists' were despoiling the cathedral and mounted officers arrested them. On another occasion, police were unable to find a suspect who was hidden among piles of pallets. A mounted officer, from his special vantage point, could peer over the fence, spot the man and direct colleagues, who then made an arrest. Success in such particular circumstances is not enough on its own to justify horses, so instead we can point to the hundreds of arrests made every year by mounted officers in the course of routine duties.

Mounted officers and their horses are most visible to the majority of people at ceremonial events, often seen by millions on TV, as well as the assembled throngs. The Met in London has rather more of this type of duty than other forces, some of it daily, like marshalling road traffic and tourists at the Changing of the Guard at Buckingham Palace; some of it at unique national events attracting international interest, such as the Notting Hill Carnival.

Mounted Police are often the top and tail of the procession on great occasions – for example, escorting HM the Queen at the annual Trooping of the Colour. Leading the way at a royal wedding or a state funeral requires the most exact timing; any slight deviation from the plans can have a disastrous effect on ceremonial coaches, cavalry, marching soldiers and whoever else may be in a long procession relying on the Mounted Police up front.

Such work has a fringe benefit in PR, and some duties may seem to be entirely PR, like school visits, until a police officer follows his instincts and relieves a boy of a knife in the playground. No arrests are likely at the highly popular Activity Ride (see pages 168–73) which, it is hoped, will return soon to public showgrounds, but even here there is a double benefit in developing the skills of both horse and rider, all otherwise normal operational members of the Mounted Branch. The Ride is a public display, an entertainment, but it demonstrates perfect timing, total commitment, professionalism and complete trust between partners as they jump through fire and solid-looking paper walls, go bareback over obstacle courses and charge across the field in crossovers and manoeuvres that would make the Red Arrows envious.

The Metropolitan Police has, as one would expect, the largest Mounted Unit in the UK, with around 140 officers and 120 horses based at seven operational stables across London. The Greater Manchester, West Yorkshire and Merseyside forces also have large Mounted sections. Numbers reflect the size of the city, obviously. More importantly, they reflect the many duties those officers and horses perform, and the many benefits that, by any common-sense analysis, the city could not manage without.

There are disadvantages, of course. Officers and animals are often exposed to bad weather with no immediate prospect of shelter. Horses can only carry one officer at a time. The animals are vulnerable to attack. Compared to cars, they are slow over longer distances. And they leave manure behind. Even so, Mounted Units keep going for reasons that are appreciated, understood and applauded, without necessarily being susceptible to the kind of statistical scrutiny accountants might prefer.

Extract from the Baltimore (Maryland) Police Department Newsletter, 1971:

The 'personal' needs of the horses are not overlooked. In the summer time, when the animal has completed his tour of duty, he is groomed and then given a cooling shower before being fed. The diet of the Department's horses is surprisingly varied to provide maximum nourishment. The staple food, of course, is hay and 5 bales are used daily to provide for the

17 animals. In addition, each feed box is filled with approximately 3 quarts of oats per day. Several times a week, the hostlers prepare what could be considered a gourmet meal for their charges, 'sweet feed'. This is a mixture of oats and corn held together with molasses. Aside from providing a pleasant treat for the animals, it's packed with needed vitamins and minerals to insure health and well-being.

They are regularly examined by a Veterinarian, provided with shots to prevent infection and given dental and eye examinations. The Department gets its horses from several sources. Some are donated. Others are purchased from area farms on trial, with a 30-day option. For a month his rider trains him and rides him in the downtown area. This gives the officer the opportunity to evaluate the animal to insure his fitness for police work in a noisy city.

In addition to a good disposition and health, size is an important element of selection. Policemen are larger than jockeys, and their jobs more rigorous than that of many cowboys; the combined weight on the horse's back, including rider, saddle and police equipment, is approximately 260 pounds (118 kilos). Each police officer-rider is an expert horseman; most have ridden since childhood. In addition, the officers are all men of experience in regular police work, each having spent years in various districts before assignment to the Mounted Division.

Times are hard and budgets are a priority. Forces that have closed their Mounted sections can still have big events that require them to get horses from somewhere. The City of London force has helped the Met sometimes with large demonstrations. No police force can be completely covered and self-sufficient all the time. Demonstrations and football don't stop just because the police have budget cuts.

Chief Inspector Helen O'Sullivan is the Senior Mounted Officer at the Met, in charge of operations and training: 'Mounted police officers are a necessary and vital requirement for ceremonial events, in particular for facilitating military troop movements safely and effectively. They often have to stop or direct traffic and in doing so must remain vigilant to prevent and detect crime. The troops that are escorted do not have the powers of a constable; they are not trained and are not there for that purpose. The officers who perform this function will have received an intelligence briefing that included details of the current threat and risk, perhaps from fixated individuals who could cause problems. The presence of mounted police officers acts as a deterrent to individuals with criminal intent and offers reassurance to the crowds of onlookers. One recent incident had a man armed with a knife outside the Palace, who was intercepted by mounted units.'

Clearly, the science and tactics of such security have developed a great deal since the two IRA bombs exploded, 20 July 1982, in Regent's Park, where seven bandsmen of the Royal Green Jackets were killed and many more spectators and bandsmen were injured, and Hyde Park. The Hyde Park weapon, a vicious nail bomb, killed four of the Queen's Life Guards (Blues and Royals), and seven of the Guards' horses, and injured all of the other soldiers and many bystanders.

PC John Davies was riding police horse Echo, escorting the Guards from Knightsbridge Barracks to Horse Guards Parade in South Carriage Drive, approaching Apsley Gate, when the bomb, in a parked car, was detonated remotely as the band marched past. Echo was wounded in the neck, eye and side, while Davies had wounds in the arm and shoulder, from which he made a full recovery.

Echo was the most sweet natured and amiable of horses, and although he mended well physically, the shock left him too nervous of traffic and crowds of people to continue his duties. He was retired to The Horse Trust in 1983, where he lived for 20 more years, to die of recurring colic aged 33, in December 2003.

From Changing the Guard, which takes place daily, to other significant ceremonial events that bring tourists into the capital, such as the State Opening of Parliament, State Visits and Trooping the Colour, without the Mounted Branch the form of these events and the policing requirement would be very different. And as for the football...

One of the newer threats the police have had to face is from away supporters in European matches. London clubs are always involved in these tournaments. London fans are used to the Mounted Police presence and generally behave accordingly, but with some of the teams they play, flares and firecrackers seem to be normal equipment for the fans to bring with them. The police train their horses with petrol bombs but this is a different kind of attack, when people bent on causing trouble throw smoking flares directly at the horse and officer.

Clearly there's a limit to what can be expected of customs searches when thousands of foreign football fans arrive in a short space of time, perhaps bringing flares and coloured smoke bombs to set off in the ground. Whether or not there's malice aforethought towards the police, it happens, and increasingly, so therefore must be planned for and trained for.

As well as reacting to new threats, the Mounted Branch must also develop and innovate in other forms of crowd control. They engage with marchers and protesters more than they used to years ago. The aim is always to prevent trouble, to stop it before it starts, and close involvement with organisers well ahead of any march or demo is essential.

PC Martin Lindsley and his partner Reg, an eight-year-old Shire cross, only three weeks into the job, were on routine patrol in Middlesbrough when a radio alert was received about a 28-year-old fugitive who had been seen by other officers. The man was wanted after failing to appear in court to answer charges concerned with a number of offences.

PC Lindsley spotted him quickly, rode up to him and dismounted. The man said, 'I'm really sorry about this,' and ran away, which the constable found most unusual as, in his experience, people tend not to run from police horses.

Reg was facing in the wrong direction and by the time PC Lindsley had him turned around and mounted, the suspect was well ahead. In full view of many shoppers and bystanders, Reg set off after his target, he and his rider on the main road while the wanted man ran along the pavement.

The man appeared to be tiring but the pursuit had to weave through busy traffic, and it was about a mile before the chase ended. The fugitive turned a corner but could only stagger into a pub car park. He doubled back but the horse and rider caught up. The man then vomited, and said, 'I'm never going to run from a police horse ever again.'

The smallest Mounted section in the UK is being closed (in 2013) in an attempt to make financial savings.

Humberside Police were spending £500,000 a year on six horses, four officers and two other staff. The stables will be sold, the six people are to be redeployed and the six horses will go to retirement or new owners.

Only a quarter of police forces in England and Wales maintain a Mounted Unit, the Chief Constable pointed out. While Humberside makes regular use of Mounted patrols, the expense of maintaining the unit cannot be justified when mounted officers from neighbouring forces can be brought in on the few occasions when they are an operational necessity. 'Sentiment has come up against austerity,' he said, and hard decisions had to be made.

At a meeting of the Cleveland Police and Crime Panel, concerns and regret were voiced by members at the decision (also in 2013) to close the Mounted section. Members said that Mounted Police were essential for crowd control at Boro home matches, and there was more to it than money: police horses were the best PR asset the Force had. People enjoy seeing them while they conduct vital duties. The amount being saved had been reported as £88,000 a year but the police would have to pay to bring horses in for special occasions.

It was understood that most of the remaining Mounted Units in England and Wales have been considered for closure since the 2010 Comprehensive Spending Review.

The Police Chief of Charleston, South Carolina pointed out the downtime necessary on either side of a Mounted-Police shift: 'When we started to look at that, it was a lot less expensive for us to operate bicycles and electric vehicles than it was to maintain the housing and feeding and care for the animals.'

Deputy Chief Constable Rod Hansen of the Gloucestershire Police is the national lead officer on mounted work, chairing the committee of representatives of all the Mounted Units, part of the Conflict Management grouping of police concerns that also includes dogs, firearms, body armour and underwater search.

'One common perception is that Mounted Police are a luxury, when in fact they are very utilitarian. If you take the Met, where we have had new studies done to give us the figures, 60 per cent of activity is on patrol – which of course is the traditional role of Mounted Police. The amount of deployments to major events varies with demand, between 11 per cent and 20 per cent, with football always providing a certain amount of business. The rest is accounted for by ceremonial duties and community work.

'That gives you the range, from Polo mints in the playground to routine policing, to front-line commitments in full body armour, to counter-terrorism, to crowd management. An officer on a horse is a marker for a crowd – there's the exit, there's the focal point – and the horses mean there is less need for coppers to order people about, or "assertive policing" as it's called. Passive policing is better, and a Mounted presence has a therapeutic effect – calmness and confidence rather than confrontation and challenge.

'The stats show that the more horses there are at the football, the less disorder there will be, and the very fact of having horses there increases the probability of arrests being made. Harder to measure are things like visibility – an officer up there on a horse – translating into an actual increase in public trust, but we expect our Oxford University study to give us some answers on such topics. Certainly our routine monthly surveys on public satisfaction and confidence suggest that both these factors increase with – and after – a Mounted presence. There is even a suggestion that people are more likely to remember seeing a mounted officer rather than a normal beat bobby, and so there is a better perception of a police presence in their locality.

'Still, people complain that they never see a police officer except going past in a car. At night in the towns, or in rural areas, mounted officers are walking police stations. The great shame is that we don't seem to be able to afford more of them.

'The new Police and Crime Commissioners are often sensitive to this, and to the public's general opinion that four legs is a good thing. However, we must admit that finances are dictating a decline. Police forces are getting rid of their horses on the assumption that they can buy in Mounted assistance when they need it. But at what point do we shrink beyond the national capability of supply meeting demand?

'Already we have vast tracts of the country where there are no Mounted Police, and there has been no geographical logic in the sequence of units closing down. Transporting horses over long distances is not easy in itself and, when they get there, ideal facilities cannot be expected. One thought we have for the future is that maybe individual Forces will not have their own Mounted Branches, but regional hubs will be formed, so that the most likely and pressing needs can be met efficiently, and the less frequent but often bigger one-off requirements can also be dealt with at a reasonable cost.

'We shall have to see what the Oxford report says. I am optimistic myself – I think the analysis will show that

Mounted Police are worth the money, more than worth it, and that positive facts will replace opinion in the arguments.'

The police, like the National Health Service, can never deal equally with everything and everyone. Resources are finite, demands are infinite, and of great importance is the public's perception of how this impossible difficulty is being met. Perhaps it is the case, then, that where big cuts in budgets must be made, one way of economising would be to increase the numbers of Mounted Police, not decrease them.

Chapter Two

What Makes
a Merlin?

What makes a police horse can never be a precisely defined list of attributes, as a Metropolitan Police scout had to point out while recommending a circus performer for training. That the horse, called Lorcan, was physically fit could not be doubted – he'd had four years touring in shows, doing all sorts of tricks, including side walking with his legs crossed.

Side walking is something the police teach, but not quite like that, and a single police officer on the back is preferred to a cargo of ballet dancers.

Lorcan provided a particular challenge to the training school. Many of the new students at the Met's school, Imber Court in Thames Ditton, have little habits and peccadilloes that need to be trained out, but Lorcan might have been expected to be the first to react to a crowd as if he was an equine Fred Astaire.

One of his specialities had been rearing up with the dancers on board, but with many hours of patient kindness from his trainers he learned that this was not the usual modus operandi for a police horse. In fact, he only went into his trick routines when so instructed, so his trainers and police riders had to be sure that whatever they did or said bore no relation to those instructions.

In his new life, based at West Hampstead, Lorcan can meet people, which he obviously likes, and out on patrol he gets at least some of the attention and acclaim that stars of the stage are used to; even more so at big events like the Diamond Jubilee, the Olympic Games and the Notting Hill Carnival. He is also good at the less public kind of police work, as he showed when helping to catch a runaway burglar.

In 1895, to join the Metropolitan Police, a man had to be over 21 and under 27 years of age, 5ft 9in tall without shoes or stockings, able to read well and write legibly with a fair knowledge of spelling, generally intelligent and free from any bodily complaint. The bodily complaints for which candidates were rejected included flat feet, stiffness of joints, narrow chest and deformities of the face.

Below is an excerpt from *The Training of Cavalry Remount Horses: A New System* by Captain Louis Edward Nolan of the 15th Hussars, written in 1852. Nolan was the officer who, during the Crimean War, carried the famously confusing message from Lord Raglan to Lord Lucan that resulted in the Charge of the Light Brigade at Balaclava, 25 October 1854; having asked permission to join the charge, he was killed in that fatal enterprise.

In those days, there was much more use of the whip which, Nolan saw, could be overdone in the urgent need to train for battle but which he believed, according to the Army's priorities, was necessary. Entry standards for horses were not so high; the Army, under severe pressure, could not be choosy. Here we are near the beginning of training:

Before commencing the bending lessons, it is well to give the horse a preparatory one of obedience, and to make him sensible of the power that man has over him. This first act of submission, which may appear of but slight importance, will prove of great service. It makes the horse quiet, and gives him confidence, and gives the man such ascendancy as to prevent the horse at the outset from resisting the means employed to bring him under control. Two lessons of half an hour each will suffice to obtain this first act of obedience from the horse.

Go up to him, pat him on the neck, and speak to him; then taking the bit-reins at a few inches from the rings with the left hand, place yourself so as to offer as much resistance as possible to the horse when he tries to break away; take the whip in the full of the right hand, with the point down, raise it quietly and tap the horse on the chest, on which he will naturally try to escape from the punishment, and rein back to avoid the whip; follow the horse whilst backing, pulling at the same time against him, but without discontinuing the application of the whip in the same quiet way, showing no signs of anger or any indications of giving in.

The horse, soon tired of trying to avoid the infliction by backing, will endeavour to do so in another way; he will rush forward, and then you must at once stop using the whip and make much of him.

This repeated once or twice will prove wonderfully successful even in the first lesson.

The horse, having found out how to avoid the punishment, will not wait for the application of the whip, but anticipate, by moving up at the slightest gesture; this will be of the greatest assistance in the subsequent bending lessons, as also of great use in mounting and dismounting, and in every way accelerate the training of the horse.

There are various ways of classifying *Equus caballus* – loosely translated, 'the horse that is for burdens', as opposed to *Equus przewalskii*, the wild horse of Mongolia, or *Equus africanus asinus*, the horse that is a donkey. The further you get into the detail with *caballus*, the less agreement you can generally find. There are probably as many breeds and varieties as there are of dog and, since crossbreeds and hybrids are just as easily produced as a labradoodle or a lurcher, there are many ways in which to get lost.

From the practical point of view – and the police are very practical people – the best way of looking at The Horse is according to the uses to which we humans put him, and straightaway we can see at least three distinct types.

The biggest, strongest and heaviest of all are the draught horses, the Shires, the Clydesdales, the Suffolk Punches, also called the 'coldbloods'. These are massive animals, sometimes 18 hands high – which is to say, 72 inches, or six feet, or 183 centimetres (a hand being four inches or 10.16 centimetres) from the ground to the withers. 'Withers' is the name for the ridge between the shoulder blades, or the spinous process of the fifth thoracic vertebra, if you want to be technical. It's used as a measuring point, being one of the few bits of a horse that doesn't move in relation to the ground.

Draught horses are slow, steady, built for work, long in stamina, usually of even temper, loyal, and tolerant of the burdens we put on them – and no good at all for racing, where we find the saddle horses. The raciest are the 'hotbloods', the light-legged thoroughbreds and Arabs, speedy and spindly – and no good at all for work.

The lightest and speediest of these saddle horses are also no good for jumping and so, with some heavy-horse influence in their background, a sub-division of the saddle horse is the hunter, the steeple-chaser, which can carry a rider far and fast across country and, consequently, must be comfortable to ride, a characteristic not required of entrants in The Derby and the 2000 Guineas.

This type of horse, the hunter, like all types much less common than they used to be, formed the breeding lines for the military, producing cavalry chargers and extra-strong versions for pulling field guns and ambulances. The chargers of olden days, used in knightly jousts, were not like those of the hussars and dragoons, being much more akin to the Shire and the Clydesdale, having to carry men dressed in heavy metal.

In between the draught horse and the thoroughbred we have the harness horses, once the most common of all. The best known of these as a distinct breed is the Hackney, favoured by Sherlock Holmes's cabby, but we must also include all those many kinds of carriage horse, stagecoach puller, lively trotter in the cart-shafts for Jane Austen characters, and the even livelier trotter still to be seen racing at Musselburgh and Appleby New Fair.

To complicate matters further, harness horses and hunters can be put together in a group called 'warmbloods', the middleweights, and those of that group measuring below 14½ hands are usually called ponies, not to be confused with the separate pony breeds such as Shetland, Fell, Dartmoor and so on. Historically, breeding the middleweights of course followed the market. Where cavalry mounts were wanted, horses were bred for that purpose. Some agricultural work was best suited to a horse rather lighter than a Shire. As tractors replaced farm horses, more people took up recreational riding so this became a breeding priority.

Looking at a warmblood, middleweight, hunter-type horse, we can see ancestral signs of both the draught horse and the thoroughbred, but no one tries to cross a Suffolk Punch directly with a flat-race champion to make a hunter – or a police horse. The genes are sufficiently embedded for middleweights to mate with middleweights, with draught horse or thoroughbred mares and stallions introduced from time to time to strengthen the blood lines. It is here that we can trace Merlin's origins.

Merlin, like many of his colleagues in the Met, came from Ireland. Usually, the Met is looking for the equine equivalent of labradoodles, mixtures the Irish call 'sport horses'. They are the offspring of two hunters, or are perhaps half or three-quarter bred – half or three-quarters thoroughbred, half or a quarter draught horse. For the Met, they must be no smaller than 16.1 hands, combining the spirit of a racer with the strength and stability of a working horse, and with good legs and feet. Like a bobby on the beat, a police horse can be on his feet all day long.

The main composite breeds of the Irish Sport Horse are the Irish Draught and the Thoroughbred, in varying proportions. In recent years, there has also been an infusion of Continental Warmblood breeds, helping to give the Irish Sport Horse its unique and much sought-after characteristics of strength, intelligence, athleticism, versatility and excellent temperament, being light-footed, balanced and supple, with good self-carriage and impulsion from the hindquarters.

Kingston Riding School was the intermediary with Merlin (or 'Lightning' as he was known to his friends), bringing him over from County Cork and keeping him at the School for a week before he moved on to Imber Court, the Met's training centre in Surrey, in the spring of 2009. Merlin's trainer, Jo Sullivan, knew a little about the horse before she met him, having asked questions about his age and health, if he'd been ridden – and what kind of riding, if he'd done any road work, how much and on what kind of roads. Merlin had been hunted, which is good for a pupil police horse. It means the horse is used to other horses, accustomed to being ridden across varied ground, and is probably fairly fit.

Although he was called Lightning, the name on his registry papers was Drive Me Quick. No name for sire or dam was given, not that such a thing matters when you can look at the horse and see for yourself that he's a magnificent animal.

When trainer and horse were introduced, there was an appraisal, first impressions, looking for positives.

Jo Sullivan: 'You want them to be brave, courageous, biddable, willing. Courage is difficult to judge, because it's quite foreign to a horse's nature. In the wild, or with an untrained domestic horse, if the choice is between fight or flight, the horse will choose flight every time. The head will go up, adrenalin will flow, the breathing will change rhythm, and off he goes. So, at this point in the process, we are looking for training potential. Can we train this animal to stop and consider, pause and evaluate, rather than panic? Will this horse be willing to leave the decision to his rider?

'A horse sees himself as in charge of his own actions. We are going to ask him to share that responsibility, first of all with me, his trainer, and then with his police rider. This is a very big thing for a horse to do, and when I first meet a young recruit, just off the boat, I can't ever be sure that he'll do it. Informed guesswork, practised eye, gut feeling and all that, but nobody could ever be sure.

'You don't really look for negatives in a young horse. The younger they are, the more you're willing to accept behaviours that might otherwise be a no-no, like rearing up on their hind legs. Merlin was four years old – the youngest I've had was three and half. They can't really be any younger than that. You can't do anything with them until they're at least three.

'That circus horse we had, Lorcan, he could do the rearing up and the criss-crossing his legs, but only if he was told to do it. If you tapped him in a certain way, he'd do the trick, but he wouldn't do it just generally walking down the road. So we had to tell his riders not to tap him in those certain ways or they'd set him off and they'd be in the act.'

This is an important point. Training a police horse takes the animal beyond becoming a good mount. Training a civilian horse to be ridden, even training him to do tricks or to perform in the dressage ring, does not require him to overcome all his natural instincts. Yes, a police horse must be responsive in horse-riding terms to every little command, and he must do so to a light touch. He must reach that stage where a novice would be unable to ride him, because he would be so responsive to the slightest movement. But, and it's a very big but, he must also overcome the fear that goes back to his prehistoric ancestors: the fear of prey animals. There are no tigers in Thames Ditton, but the freshman horse doesn't know that.

John Solomon Rarey was a famous 19th-century 'horse whisperer' from Ohio, USA. In his book *The Complete Horse Tamer and Farrier*, 1862, he set out three fundamental principles:

First. That any horse may be taught to do any thing a horse can do, if taught in a proper manner.

Second. That a horse is not conscious of his own strength until he has resisted and conquered a man, and that, by taking advantage of man's reasoning powers, a horse can be handled in such a manner that he shall not find out his strength.

Third. That by enabling a horse to examine every object with which we desire to make him familiar, with the organs naturally used for that purpose, viz.: Seeing, smelling, and feeling, you may take any object around, over, and on him, that does not actually hurt him.

The initial phase of the training is four weeks but someone with Jo's experience can tell in the first week if a horse is going to make it, and most of that time is spent indoors, in the school. Merlin didn't try to remove Jo from his back but he was pretty green otherwise – then again, he was a quick learner. He'd come from open fields in County Cork, a life of ease with the occasional outing, tearing across country at the hunt. Walking around, inside an empty building, was an entirely new experience.

Jo Sullivan: 'If horses come in that have had a bit of schooling, they're generally very good on the lunge rein. Merlin was hopeless. He had absolutely no idea, but he was good on the voice. I could speak to him in a calming way and it would relax him, comfort him, and reassure him when he was on the right lines. Eventually you would want him to understand voice commands. First, we had to teach him what it was we were going to command him to do, like getting a dog to sit that doesn't yet know how to sit properly.

'Merlin didn't expect to have to walk or trot at all. He didn't know about walking in a circle. He'd been hunted in Ireland, gung-ho, going in a straight line, in hot pursuit. At first, he wanted to do the same in the stable yard and the school. He wanted to charge around our little arena like he was auditioning for the Grand National.

'When it came to the trial for his first report (see below) he still didn't know much, but he had shown that he could grasp the schooling idea, and I was quite sure he would soon get the hang of all these foreign practices I was making him try. With some horses, you can take them into the school day after day and they don't progress. They reach a point and that's it. With Merlin, every day was an improvement, better than yesterday.

'He knew when I was pleased with him. He listened to me, his ears were going; I'd pat him and speak to him. It doesn't take much, just a kind word and a "good boy", and a stroke on the neck. You could see he was taking note of that. Horses are timid animals – their natural response to trouble is to run away from it. The other side of that coin is that they enjoy affection, they enjoy kindness, and they seem to know whether it's genuine or not.

'Obviously you can't give treats while you're working, and you wouldn't want to keep stopping for that, but a handful of nuts won't go amiss at the end of a session. When we do what we call our "nuisance training", which is when we get all our tarpaulins and mattresses and cardboard boxes and whatnot, and scatter all that stuff about and make them walk over it, we do that with treats. I'd be leading Merlin, not riding the first time, and I'd tempt him over every obstacle with a few pony nuts. You know, it's decision time – I don't like the look of this horrible old mattress, but if I step over it, I'll get a little something to eat. Eat? With Merlin, that was decision made.'

'To those who understand the philosophy of horse-manship, the spirited horses are the easiest trained; for when we have a horse that is wild and lively, we can train him to our will in a very short time, for they are generally quick to learn, and always ready to obey.'

John Solomon Rarey

In 1908, the *Police Review* reported that the authorities at Scotland Yard had seriously discussed the use of dogs as the constable companion and help, and Sir Edward Henry (Commissioner), who regarded the innovation sympathetically, considered the only crucial objection to be the sentimental prejudices of the public.

Some chief constables were concerned about using

animals that could bite as a means of upholding the law, and were worried about the consequences in liability of the dogs misbehaving.

Dogs were introduced as assistants in patrol work but were found to be more useful in tracking, searching, detection and arrests. While the public could be encouraged to be friendly towards police horses, police dogs could not be trained for their work and at the same time allow themselves to be petted and stroked by strangers.

Jo Sullivan: 'You ask the dog handlers and they'll say the same: it's all done with kindness. We don't use carrot and stick, because we don't need the stick – well, very rarely. We have schooling whips, and sometimes a horse is lazy and, say, isn't keen on going forward today. You give him a little tap with the schooling whip. If you have to do it again tomorrow and the next day, you don't hit him harder. You give up and send him back, failed.

'Now, standing still. Horses do not know naturally about standing still. They don't do it in the wild, and they don't do it in an ordinary riding life, but in the police they have to do it all the time. They come up to road junctions – stop. A member of the public says excuse me – stop. The officer sees something that needs a look – stop. On ceremonial duties – stand still for ever. So, I walk beside them and get them to stop. I'd walk Merlin around the yard and stop to talk to people. If a horse won't stop for me in week one, that's it – bye bye.

'I ranked Merlin as very good at that. Well, he was good in what had become his home, his new own environment, but that was only a start. Then we walked down the quiet roads, stopping at junctions, or I'd decide just to stop anyway and stand for five minutes. It's a gradual thing, to be built up. The horse will usually think his equivalent of "This is boring". It's a reasonable reaction. Why have I got to stand here doing nothing? Then we tried it on the busier roads. Will Merlin stand with so much more going on around him? Yes, was the answer.

'But we found out he was a nibbler. He particularly liked handbags, and this is something you can't really train them not to do. He never bit anyone, and never would, and mostly people didn't mind him having a look at their shopping.'

It was clear to Jo that she had a good 'un in Merlin, and could cut back on the interview process, as it were, and start moving on with his training proper, although there was a little problem, and the solution to it was something that he, being a born chewer and nibbler, did not especially relish. He was overweight, too fat, from too much good living out in the green fields, and he had to go on a diet. His fighting weight is around 600 kilos and he was well over that.

Jo Sullivan: 'He'd been used to being turned out, and when he came here there was no turn out, no green fields. I'd have him in the school for half an hour then he'd be back in his stable. It was a very big change for him. Some of them don't adjust and have to go. Some of them don't like being alone with no other horses close by, or in there together. Some of them get agitated, not able to burn up their energy. Merlin, well, he didn't really care so long as he had some hay in front of him, which of course we were cutting down on, so he wasn't very happy with me. But he was all right with it, except for the chewing. We had to put notices up. Do not leave anything anywhere near this horse. Merlin the Mangler,

Merlin the Menace. It wouldn't matter what it was – a mobile phone, a riding hat, your cup of coffee. If he could reach it, he'd have it.'

Merlin's normal diet in training was 70/30 forage/concentrate, which translates as a bale of hay a day, or a bag of special horse silage, made from part-cured hay rather than the fermented fresh grass that farm animals have. He'd also get through a bag of pony nuts in a week, a 20-kilo bag, and his drinking water could be up to 100 pints a day (12 gallons or more, 50 or 60 litres).

Ridden training outside the school, on the roads, among the traffic, is always done in pairs, with another trainer on an experienced horse as escort. The junior rides kerbside, to start with anyway, and the senior on the outside. Usually the escort, the mentor, is a horse on the way to retirement. Escorting duties at Imber Court are a wind-down from rigorous police routine towards the life of leisure that will shortly be his reward for 15 or more years of service. Occasionally, the escort horse is there because he's had an accident that makes him unable to fulfil all the duties, or perhaps he's had a really bad experience at the football and that's made him unreliable in those situations. He can come to Imber Court and escort the novices and never have to go to football again.

Recently, the biggest police horse in Britain has handed in his uniform for the last time, after more than 10 years' duty. The horse, a thoroughbred-cross chestnut gelding called Clyde, is a massive 19 hands, but his size may have been a contributory factor to the arthritis which has forced his retirement, to be spent at the Horse Trust in Buckinghamshire.

He leaves the Cleveland Constabulary with a magnificent record in ceremonial parades and at hundreds of football matches.

A young girl was killed after horses were spooked by a woman in 1860s costume, reported the *Arizona Daily Star* in March 2007. The woman, carrying an open parasol and taking part in a parade, crossed in front of two Percheron horses pulling a wagon, causing them to bolt and run into a pony being ridden by Brielle Boisvert. The girl was knocked from her horse and trampled by the Percherons. Brielle was five years old, despite parade rules stating a minimum age of eight. The wagon driver was very experienced and, at his own request, had a mounted marshal riding beside him as he had felt one of his horses was not behaving as quietly as he would have liked.

Jo Sullivan: 'Every horse-rider knows that anything can spook a horse. It can be a noise, a light, a crisp packet, a skip parked on the road, a shadow. Sometimes, the rider doesn't see the cause at all. So, I go out on the road with a new horse, and a supermarket carrier bag blows across. The horse turns and runs. So, do you believe you'll be able to train him to think OK, that's fine, I'll keep on walking, or will he always think no, I don't care what you say, I'm running?

'The reaction you want when you meet something new is for the horse to stop, look, decide there's nothing to worry about, and walk on. Or maybe tuck in behind the escort. What you don't want is for a lorry to go past belching smoke and the horse spins away and runs off and it takes you 10 minutes to get him back under control. Or, the horse stops dead and won't move on, which can be difficult if you can't see what he's seen and is reacting to.'

The eyeballs of the horse are the largest of any land animal, and he has reasonably effective vision straight in front, raising or lowering his head to focus better on distant or near objects. His peripheral vision, one-eyed on either side, gives him the ability to see almost all the way around, with a blind spot directly behind, but it is only with one eye. Definition and distance telling are not good. In the wild, this gives him a chance of glimpsing anything that might be a predator. In domestic life, it often means that the poor human rider, with binocular vision only effective as far as the head can be turned, has no idea what invisible predators have been spotted.

The way their eyes are constructed also means that horses are not as quick as humans in adjusting to sudden light changes, as might be met in tunnels or horse boxes.

Jo Sullivan: 'Railway bridges can be a big thing. Being under one when a train goes over, with all the echoing noise in a dark archway, that can be scary, and that's where the escort horse really comes in. Coming up to it, the trainee looks up at the bridge, sees a train going over; he doesn't like it, but the escort doesn't react. The young horse gets the message in some way, that these things are not a concern. Take no notice. They play a big part, the escort horses.

'I'm saying "he", because we don't take many mares – they tend to be too argumentative. We do have some, and when they're good, they're very, very good, but they can be stubborn about certain things that put them out of police reckoning. One mare might be brilliant as a potential dressage performer but she won't put up with buses going past, and if she won't, she won't, and that's the end of it.'

'It often happened to me with a clever mare I had, that when I threw the handkerchief to some distance, I could not prevail upon her to pick it up till I threatened her with the whip, then she at once rushed off, and brought it to me.'

François Baucher, French riding master, *c.* 1840

Chapter Three

How Lightning/Drive Me Quick 2974268 Became Merlin 184

FIRST SCHOOL REPORT

An article in a 1905 edition of *Police Review* noted that PC William Hallett of Y Division had retired after 26 years as a mounted officer, having ridden 144,000 miles or more than five times around the world in the course of his duty.

'The health and condition of the horses should be carefully considered, and great care be taken not to overfatigue them by too violent exertion; punishment never being inflicted on a young horse, except for decided restiveness, and downright vice. Even in that case, your object only being to oblige him to go forward, you will, the moment he moves on, treat him kindly.

'When a horse resists, before a remedy or correction is

39

thought of, examine minutely all the tackle about him. For want of this necessary precaution, the poor animal is often used ill without reason; and being forced into despair, is in a manner, obliged to act accordingly be his temper and inclination ever so good.

'Horses are by degrees made obedient through the hope of recompense, as well as the fear of punishment. To use these two incentives with judgment is a very difficult matter, requiring much thought, much practice, and not only a good head, but a good temper; mere force, and a want of skill and coolness, tend to confirm vice and restiveness. Resistance in horses is often a mark of strength and vigor, and proceeds from high spirits; but punishment would turn it into vice.

'Weakness frequently drives horses into being vicious when any thing wherein strength is necessary is required of them. Great care should be taken to distinguish from which of these causes the opposition arises.

'It is impossible in general to be too circumspect in lessons of all kinds, for horses find out many ways and means of opposing what you demand of them. Many will imperceptibly gain a little every day on their rider; he must, however, always treat them kindly, at the same time showing that he does not fear them, and will be master.'

Captain Louis Nolan, 1852

Merlin had three school reports over the whole training period, called Remount Assessment Reports. 'Remount' is an old army word for a fresh horse brought into a cavalry regiment, or a horse replacing another that has been killed or wounded in battle. A lot of these cavalry terms have percolated into police vocabulary for historical reasons, and 'remount' here simply means a new horse in training.

At this point, Merlin had had his first four weeks of probationary training, a kind of extended practical interview. His trainer, the very experienced Jo Sullivan, began with a horse that, in her own words, 'knew nothing' – he'd been hunted but never schooled. Now, after those make-or-break four weeks, Jo had to fill in Merlin's report for the training manager, giving marks out of ten for each of 16 activities attempted: 10 scored for excellent, 9 very good, 8 good, and so on. The minimum he could have and survive was 5 for sufficient, otherwise it was down to 1 for very bad and zero for 'not performed' – that is, the horse just would not do whatever it was.

'The first thing is to teach the horse to know what you want; and you must in various little clever ways, try to make him sensible of it, before you attempt to impress it on his memory.

'Is it with blows that you will make him sensible of it? Certainly not: but make the object in view as clearly perceptible to his faculties as you possibly can: then, by punishment, or caresses, applied at the right moment, impress the movements required on his memory.'

François Baucher

Merlin had to make a good total score. Anything less than 100 out of 160 and serious questions would be asked.

His report began with three 9s, for *Health, General Temperament* – 'A really nice horse with a great attitude' – and *Tie Up and Leave*, although Jo had already learned not to leave him near anything he could chew. *Lead in Hand* (something he had obviously done before) got an 8, and he received another 8 for *Good to Groom*, which was something he had never done.

Part of the grooming process is looking at the feet. Some young horses won't ever have been shod, and will never have had their feet picked up by someone. It's been known to take weeks to get a horse to allow his feet to be picked up. Bearing in mind that a police horse is reshod every six weeks, the trainer has to decide if a horse is going to learn this or if it's always going to be a nuisance. Of course, if the trainer goes behind the horse and gets an attempted kick, which is rare, there will be no more school reports.

Merlin only got a 6, satisfactory, for *Behaviour with Farrier* – 'Good when shod outside the forge.' He didn't like the smoke inside, or the noise of the extractor fan. It's a busy place, the farrier's shop, with horses and people going past, and the horse to be shod is in there on his own. Merlin didn't object to the hot shoeing but he would rather be in the open and not confined in that dark, smelly, slightly hellish little space, if you wouldn't mind.

Trim, Clip, Pull Mane and Tail are all little temperament tests, and he got a 7, fairly good – 'Have pulled mane and tail, good, but not tested clipping' – so a technical mark down there.

Lungeing, 7 – 'Good on the voice, can get a little confused on direction changing.' Merlin was very good at recognising tones in voices, so he knew when he was doing well and when not so well. The problem was, in this early stage, that he had no clue about what he was supposed to do well.

Dynamic Ability, 7 – marks for the way he moved, was he

straight in his body, could he be turned left and right, walk, trot, canter? Galloping is not a formal part of the course, although unscheduled, unwanted galloping sometimes happens. Merlin's report said, 'Stiff to the left, has shown some nice work.' Horses generally are 'stiff' to one side or the other, which is to say they favour left or right, rather like humans being left- or right-handed.

School Manoeuvres – oh dear, a 6 – 'Green but very willing.' Merlin had to be entirely educated in school movements and was somewhat behind the ideal on this one. It was only because he was so compliant, and such a quick learner, that he got as high as a 6.

'When remount horses join a regiment, they should be distributed amongst the old horses; they thus become accustomed to the sight of saddles and accoutrements, &c., &c., and the old horses on each side of them, taking no notice of all these things inspire the young ones with confidence.

'The first day they are led out to the drill-ground in saddles and with snaffle-bridles, and the instructor should inspect the saddles to see that the cruppers and girths are rather loose, so as not to inconvenience the horses; he should then order the men to mount quietly, and at once walk them around in a large circle, and whilst so doing, divide them into squads of not more than sixteen each. He should pick out all the horses that are in poor condition, or weak, or very young, and make a squad of them, giving them less work than the others.

'The instructor should allow no shouting, nor noise in the squads, and even the words of command should be cautiously given at first, in a quiet tone of voice, so as not to startle or set off the young horses. When the squads are told off, they are filed to stables. If any of the horses are intractable, the men should dismount and lead them; but those that go quietly should be ridden to and from the drill-ground, care being taken not to allow them to close up nearer than six feet.'

Captain Louis Nolan, 1852

Travelling on Horse Box – all Merlin had to do for that was the journey from his temporary accommodation at the riding school to Imber Court, four or five miles. His trip from Ireland was not adjudicated – 'Loaded and travelled well from Kingston', 7.

Behaviour with Half Section – this was his outing in a pair with an escort, known in police jargon as 'half-section'. A section is four, abreast or in pairs – 'Excellent attitude towards other horses', 9. Merlin also received a 9 for his *General Reaction to Roads*, 'Shows excellent potential', and a good 8 for *General Reaction to Kerbside Nuisances* – 'Likes to look but keeps going forward.' Yes, he did like to look, and this trait in his character would provide some fun and games once he went on duty.

With an 8 for *Standing Still* and another 8 for *Sudden Noises*, both with 'Very good' added, Merlin scored 125 out of a possible 160. His trainer was quite sure: faced with 'This horse should/should not be purchased in my opinion', Jo deleted 'should not'.

As well as having Australia's oldest police force, New South Wales also claims to have the oldest continuous operational Mounted Unit in the world [Note: the

London Met might argue with that, see pages 192–200]. It was formed by Governor Brisbane on 7 September 1825. In comparison, say the NSW Police, the London Metropolitan Mounted Police were formed in 1829 [no, they were not, see pages 192–200] and the Royal Canadian Mounted Police in 1863.

By 1830 the NSW Force was commanded by Lieutenant-Colonel Snodgrass. In the more settled part of the colony, there were four divisions: Sydney, with the main detachment incorporating the Governor's Guard, and three covering the rural areas. By the early 1900s the Mounted Police had over 800 personnel and 900 horses. Most police stations throughout the state had Mounted Units attached to them.

The modern Unit has just under 40 (each) of officers and horses, and is equipped with iPads. Duties are defined as: public order management, including escorting arrest teams through hostile crowds, escorting ambulances and police vehicles and relieving pressure and gaining ground for the riot police; community events such as local festivals, parades and celebrations throughout the state; searches, mainly in country areas or outer suburban areas and national parks, for lost persons, escapers, drug plantations etc.; stock mustering and recapturing runaway horses; protocol (VIP escorts) and public relations; the Musical Ride at the Sydney Royal Easter Show and larger country shows.

All constables are responsible for the care and maintenance of their own saddlery, for grooming their horses and keeping the stables clean. One day a week is devoted to practice and extra training.

The next phase of training, aiming towards Merlin's second school report, the amber one, took four months. He'd done well on his first (red) report; expectations were high for the amber and the green. The big difference now was that no marks were awarded; he was expected to pass every test. It was simply a question of when. Instead of nine out of ten (or three out of ten, see me), in this case the trainer puts the date that the standard is reached.

There remains an overall quality assessment. It is possible to reach all the standards but still raise a few doubts about being fully up to the hardest jobs. Of the Met's seven operational stables, the busiest and most stressful is Great Scotland Yard. Here, the horse steps out on duty and within a few moments he is in Whitehall, Trafalgar Square, Parliament Square, thronged with traffic, heaving with tourists. Perhaps a young horse like Merlin would pass his exams but need a year or two out in a quieter district where he could mature, grow up and acquire the street wisdom that characterises the true professional.

At the bottom of the amber form, there's a box for 'Area Recommended'. If Merlin were to come out at the top, Jo Sullivan would have to write 'Any' in that box.

Jo: 'He was a lovely horse to train, very biddable, very interested in everything. He enjoyed his training, and he was the class comedian. You'd turn up in the morning and he'd be standing there with his rug over his head. Or, he'd have disrobed entirely without undoing the ties. Houdini, he was. Rugs are tied around in three places. He did it at night and we still don't know how. You'd go in with the grooming kit and he'd beat you to it. Turn your back and he'd have picked up a brush and thrown it somewhere. He was the lovable rogue.

'He could reach over his stable door and open the top bolt with his mouth. He'd learned that the bottom bolt on most of the doors, being not exactly new, would gradually slide open if the door was kicked repeatedly in a certain way. "Merlin's escaped again" soon became a regular cry around the yard, but he'd never gone far. He'd be round the corner, eating something. The first place we'd look was the feed room, but he'd go back into his stable quite happily. He wasn't at all stroppy that way, and he didn't make a fuss when we fitted an extra bolt to the stable door so he couldn't get out any more.'

There are presently 40 male officers and 12 females on the (Taipei) Mounted Police team. Their daily patrol territories cover the more populous districts in the county, extending from Danshui Fisherman's Wharf to Yingge District, which is noted for its ceramic art works, museums, and other tourist spots.

Mounted Police have the advantage of patrolling terrain districts that are difficult for the police vehicles to comb. With high mobility and extensive patrol routes, the senior officer, Captain Huang, said the Mounted Police can prevent people from attempting crimes. They can also quickly notify colleagues in patrol cars to rush to crime scenes.

Huang declined to comment if the Mounted Police's new patrol plan in the downtown area and promoting the horse image is related to the election of Ma Ying-jeou as the nation's new president. In Chinese 'Ma' means horse.

REMOUNT ASSESSMENT REPORT
(AMBER), MERLIN 184

'Good to Trim and Clip' – Merlin wasn't an especially hairy horse, but in the police he had to look smart and tidy. The feathers that grow naturally on the legs had to come off, and the method used is electric clippers.

Jo Sullivan: 'There are some horses that will not tolerate the clippers. It could be the buzzing noise; it could be they don't like the feel of the vibration. And when they grow their winter coat, all that has to come off too. And the mane, that has to be a uniform length. Some won't mind you doing the body – the clip – but won't let you do their feet – the trim – and some are the other way round. Some are just plain ticklish. Mostly they don't mind and maybe even like it, but just a few have to be distracted, with some food maybe, or with another person petting and talking.'

If that doesn't work, and everything has been tried, the trainer must call in the vet to give a light sedative. Once or twice with that, and the problem usually disappears. Jo says: 'Honestly, they have so much else to put up with in training, it's very rare that they don't soon get used to the hairdresser. But it is important, so it has to be on their report.'

First time around, Merlin took a full clip, including face, ears, all that. Next came *'Introduced to a Stall'*. Depending on circumstances, the horse will need to spend time in a single stall, where he can stand, lie down, feed, drink, but is tied to the wall in front and can't turn round. This was the old way to keep horses when off duty, when there were many more horses and space for stabling was insufficient. It has mostly been phased out and will be entirely, but it is anathema to some horses, especially when they can hear things going on behind them.

Jo: 'Even if a horse is never going to see a stall in the old sense, on duty the officers are bound to want to tie him up sometimes, for a couple of hours maybe, and expect him to stand without making a fuss.'

Perhaps the sociable Merlin would find this difficult. It was one of the last things he did on the Amber list, but he did it all right.

'*Good to Shoe and Have Reasonable Manners*' – Hot shoeing is always going to be a surprise to a young horse that's never been shod, and some will do anything and everything to avoid it. They rear up, kick out and pull away. Merlin hadn't particularly liked it at first, but was OK so long as he didn't have to go into the forge. Out in the real world, the farrier has a lot to do and a certain time to do it in. Some of what Jo calls 'young horse behaviour' has to be tolerated, but when students leave Imber Court they must be amenable to having four shoes put on in the time allocated. Here's Captain Nolan again:

'Plunging is very common amongst restive horses. If they continue to do it in one place, or backing, they must be, by the rider's legs and whip firmly applied, obliged to move forward; but, if they do it flying forward, keep them back, and ride them gently, and very slow, for a good time together. Of all bad tempers in horses, that which is occasioned by harsh treatment and ignorant riders is the worst.

'Rearing is a bad vice, and, in weak horses, especially, a dangerous one; whilst the horse is up, the rider must yield the hand, and at the time he is coming down again, he must vigorously determine him forward; if this be done at any other time but when the horse is coming down, it may add a spring to his rearing, and make him come over. If this fails you must make the horse move on by getting some one on foot to strike him behind with a whip. With a good hand on them, horses seldom persist in this vice, for they are themselves much afraid of falling backward. When a horse rears, the man should put his right arm around the horse's neck, with the hand well up, and close under the horse's gullet; he should press his left shoulder, forward, so as to bring his chest to the horse's near side; for if the horse fall back, he will then fall clear.'

Captain Louis Nolan, 1852

In 2003 the Houston Police Department Mounted Patrol was the first unit in the US to initiate a barefoot programme, and they say it has proved to be a success. They no longer use farriers and claim to have had very few hoof problems. Mounted officers are trained in barefoot hoof trimming. At first, when a horse's hooves are trimmed, hoof boots are used. Gradually the hooves will strengthen and no longer need the boots.

Possibly this will enable mounted officers to approach difficult situations more stealthily, but surely the sound of the iron shoes on the ground is part of that characteristic 'police presence'?

'Has Worked in Both Schools' – now this was a test of mettle. Not used to any kind of schooling or work indoors, Merlin had become accustomed to the small riding hall. He was happy in there, but he had to step up to the big school –

Olympic-size, you might say – with a completely different look and feel to it. There were all kinds of things going on all around, with other horses, more people, shouts, talk – all very busy and, at first, quite scary too.

As with all schools, there has to be break-time, or playtime, here called 'loose schooling'. The saddle and bridle are taken off, and the horse is free to do what he wants.

Jo Sullivan: 'They trot round, buck, roll in the sand, whatever. It's a release of tension, mostly, mental and muscular. The disciplined schooling we do nearly every day is the equivalent of a young child doing the three Rs. A bit of steam has to be let off. Most of them need no encouragement; Merlin certainly didn't. You want to see them trotting around, all nice and loose, head down, but if one stands there not understanding, you might have to push him a bit, get him to trot about with the lunge whip.'

Police horses are being prepared for urban life. There's no turn-out, as most civilian horses have; loose schooling takes the place of turn-out as a relaxant. But do the horses want to go back to school after that?

Jo: 'If they were feeling tense, they've lost that with their bit of a romp so they've had their coffee break, as it were, and back to work is what they expect. They can't fool about at work, so we give them fooling-about time in between.'

A HORSE'S PRAYER

Give me food and drink, and care for me when the day's work is done. Shelter me, give me a clean bed and leave me not too small a place in the stable. Talk to me, for your voice often takes the place of reins; be good to me and I will serve you yet more gladly and love you. Don't tear at the reins; don't reach for your whip when we come to a hill. Don't beat me or hit me if I misunderstand you but give me time to understand. Don't think me disobedient if I fail to do your will; perhaps there is something amiss with my harness or my hooves. Check my teeth when I don't eat; perhaps I have a bad tooth, and you know that hurts. Don't tether me too tight and don't crop my tail, my only weapon against mosquitoes and flies.

When the day comes, dear master, when I'm no longer any use to you, don't let me starve or freeze, nor sell me. Don't give me to a stranger who might not care for me as you have, but be kind-hearted, as I would be to you.

Anonymous

Officers with the Metropolitan Police Mounted Branch breathed a sigh of relief when their oldest-serving horse returned to duty after a life-threatening illness. Zena returned to Great Scotland Yard's stables after fighting off colic – a twisting of the gut ailment that kills thousands of animals each year.

Officers had feared the worst when the 20-year-old grey mare became seriously ill. A vet was quickly called to the stables and concluded Zena's life was in danger. It was believed that she might not survive major surgery because of her age, but she proved to be tough, responding miraculously well to pain-killing medication. After a short rest, Zena returned to duty.

Inspector Chris Turner of the Mounted Branch

admitted he was thrilled with the horse's return. He said: 'Zena has an outstanding history of courage and ability and is always first into the fray leading the way – including the Parliament Square student disorder in December 2010, where she played a pivotal role.'

Mounted Branch rider PC Tamaris Vaughan was equally thrilled. She added: 'Zena has led the way in everything from the Royal Wedding, as part of the Grey Escort, to helping public order officers' progress during the summer disturbances [of August 2011]. I'm thrilled to welcome her back and will make sure I treat her to some of her favourite mints the next time we are out on duty.'

'Has Been Ridden in Remount Ride and Accepted All Nuisances' – A great deal of the training of a police horse is about desensitising the animal to his natural instincts. It has to be a slow and gentle process; there must be no overload because weeks and months of work can be lost in a few seconds by pushing a horse too far, and the greatest danger of that happening is in the remount ride, the name given to formal circuits and manoeuvres, with and without nuisances and obstacles, in the indoor school. There are many remount rides that a horse must go through.

The general format is to have three trainees (remounts) and one old lag as babysitter in, at first, the small riding school. To help them learn to work together in a confined space, they perform various simple manoeuvres, in fours (a section), in pairs (half section) or in line (directed by a senior trainer in military style): right turn all together, walk in a wide circle, walk in a tight circle, take a turn at the front of the line, at the back of the line, go from walk to trot to walk.

Initially, a new horse's reactions are all dictated by what the other horses do. Teaching a horse disciplined behaviour in a group and teaching him to work on his own are equally foreign to his instincts. One horse breaking rhythm can set the others off. Into half sections, slow walk, up to canter on left rein, repeat on right rein, move into a section, move into single file, left wheel, right wheel – the riders of course are very experienced and skilful, being trainers from the school and serving officers, but every horse has a first time for everything.

'In working on a straight line, the horse's head remains placed to the front, and the rider will bear his bridle-hand to the right or left and press the opposite leg, according to the hand he wishes to strike his horse off to; and he must carefully avoid throwing his horse's forehand roughly to either side.

'In the last fourteen days, you perfect the horses in all their preceding lessons, and bring them to work steadily and well at a canter, including changes of leg, half-passage, accustoming them to sights and sounds, &c., &c.

'Be careful to shorten the walking and trotting lessons in proportion as you increase the cantering. Trot for a few minutes; then the Bending Lessons, short but not hurried; and at once to the Cantering, which is now the chief object.

'Of course, it is unnecessary to remind the Instructor that reining back and the use of the spur, as well as going about on the forehand and haunches, should be practised, as opportunity offers, during the whole lesson.

'When cantering, never cease making the men work to

'All horses have their own characters, and if a long-term relationship is to flower, horse and rider must be compatible.' PC Karen Howell and Merlin on duty outside Buckingham Palace.

(© *Bob Langrish*)

Antecedents: (*Above left*) an officer of the Dockyard Police *c.*1900 – swords were still sometimes carried by the Mounted Branch until the 1920s. (*Centre*) Officers of the Mounted Branch's J Division in the first decade of the 20th century. (*Below*) a mounted officer helps to escort a shipment of gold bullion through Poplar, East London, in 1911.

(*All MPS*)

(*Above left*) Charlie, a twice-wounded veteran of the First World War, and the first horse across the Hindenburg Line during the final push against the Germans in September 1918, with his rider, PC Perkins, *c.* 1919. (*MPS*)

(*Above right*) Billy, hero of the 1923 Cup Final between Bolton Wanderers and West Ham United, with his rider, PC George Scorey. (*MPS*)

(*Below*) Billy helping to clear the crowd from the pitch before the match at the then new Wembley Stadium – in the age of monochrome photography, Scorey's grey mount stood out, and to this day the match is remembered as the 'white horse final'. (*Getty Images*)

(*Above*) Training in crowd control between the wars – some of the 'protestors' waving hats and flags and beating drums appear to be Guardsmen, and others police officers.

(*Centre*) When Sir Oswald Mosley's British Union of Fascists attempted to march through London's East End in October 1936, the local population rose up in protest, resulting in what came to be called 'the Battle of Cable Street'. Officers of the Mounted Branch were called in to restore order.

(*Below*) 'They take the jumps, waving their saddles in the air' – the Mounted Branch's highly popular Activity Ride, here photographed in the 1960s.   (*All MPS*)

(*Above*) 'In our training, we are taught to advance at a pace that indicates we are not going to stop… It's a rehearsed move, called a "dispersal", and it's always supported by foot police.' To any would-be rioter, it's an impressive sight.   (*MPS*)

(*Below left*) One of the Mounted Branch's duties is to escort the Queen's Life Guards – in this case, a detachment of the Blues and Royals – on daily ceremonial duties. The presence of other horses can be unnerving for inexperienced police horses.

(*Alastair Macdonald/REX*)

(*Below right*) PC Karen Howell and Merlin with her husband, Sergeant Rob Howell on Lionheart, inside the stables at Great Scotland Yard.   (*PC Karen Howell*)

(*Above left*) PC Howell mucking out Merlin's stall at Great Scotland Yard, and (*above right*) sponging his eyes, part of the daily routine of tending to her mount.

(*Below*) Riding out of the police stables at Great Scotland Yard to go on patrol.

(*All © Bob Langrish*)

(*Right and centre*) A study in contrasts: PC Howell and Merlin on public-order duties outside Buckingham Palace, and in full riot gear.

(*Below*) It takes a very well-trained horse and a very competent rider to cope with traffic duties, here in the Mall close to the Victoria Memorial in front of Buckingham Palace.

(*All © Bob Langrish*)

(*Above left*) Merlin's first encounter with a military band caused him to leap into the air. Not now: here he and PC Howell escort the band of the Irish Guards as it marches out of the front entrance to Buckingham Palace. (© *Bob Langrish*)

(*Above right*) 'The police horse that stacks traffic cones' – in fact, Merlin's trick began as an attempt to eat one of the cones … (© *Bob Langrish*)

(*Below*) 'We walked down the Mall with what seemed like the whole world following': Karen and Merlin (centre) helping to lead the vast crowd along The Mall to Buckingham Palace after Prince William's wedding, 29 April 2011.

(*Sipa Press/REX*)

collect the pace; the more collected it is, the better. The leading files are the men to look to. Never keep a man at the head of a squad who cannot collect his horse to any pace required of him; it makes the greatest difference in the bringing on of the horses.

'Look to the position of the men's hands, and their seats on horseback, get their legs close, and prevent them from sticking out stiffly and away from the horse's sides, which is a great though very common fault: elbows back, hands low, the lower the better, and close to the body, heads up, and heels down; all this contributes greatly to assist the horse in his work.

'Practise the sabre exercise (attack and defence), first at a walk, until the horses are steady, and when doing it at a canter. If any of them show symptoms of fear, the men should return to guard immediately, quiet them, and try it again.'

Captain Louis Nolan, 1852

After half an hour or so of manoeuvres, it's time to introduce the 'nuisances'; this has to be done very carefully and with considerable cunning. One little trick, for instance, is to use a flag as a grooming tool, so the horse gets used to this before it is waved in his face. Even then, it may be the motion of the flag that spooks the horse, or the swishing noise it makes. As with every nuisance, if the horse is unhappy, the trainers go back and start again from a slightly different direction.

The horse is the barometer, the gauge of how far to go. When it came to flags, Merlin just wanted to eat it, so that was fine.

Objects on the ground – mattresses, tyres, tarpaulins, sheets of cardboard – all look strange and alarming to a new horse, and he will always want to go round rather than over. When he does go over, the thing makes a funny noise, different to the sand of the school floor, and if that's not enough, here comes someone shaking a big plastic bottle with gravel in it, and there's someone else banging a five-gallon drum with a stick.

'There's somebody in front waving Dr Death, and somebody behind hitting a riot shield with another stick. Should I turn to look, or should I keep walking towards the mad fool with the scarecrow?' (The scarecrow is a copy of the Grim Reaper dummy used by G8 protesters in London.)

As the horses walk forward in a section, four abreast, the assistants throw plastic balls at them. If one decides to backpedal, the others will very likely follow suit. Later, when they go to Gravesend for their advanced training, it won't be plastic balls they'll be having thrown at them. Coming forward in section at the canter, there will be petrol bombs going off 10 metres in front.

Jo Sullivan: 'In the nuisance training, you put a tarpaulin down and see if the horse will walk over it. Most horses are cautious and need to be tempted with food. Merlin picked the tarpaulin up and threw it to the side. We had a shopping trolley in there. He didn't care – bang, it was out of the way. Flags waving, guns going off, nothing bothered him. If you put something in his path, he'd either eat it or chuck it. And that was obviously something in his character that he would never lose.'

'Starting often proceeds from a defect in the sight, which, therefore, must be carefully looked into. Whatever the horse is afraid of, bring him up to it gently, and if you make much of him every step he advances, he will go quite up to it by degrees, and soon grow familiar with all sorts of objects. Nothing but great gentleness can correct this fault; for, if you inflict punishment, the dread of chastisement causes more starting than the fear of the object; if you let him go by the object without bringing him in to it, you increase the fault, and encourage him in his fear.

'However, if a horse turns back, you must punish him for doing so, and that whilst his head is away from the object; then turn him, and ride him quietly up toward what he shied at, and make much of him as long as he moves on; never punish him with his head to the object, for if you do he is as badly off with his head one way as the other, whereas, when the horse finds out that he is only punished on turning back, he will soon give it up. If a horse takes you up against a wall and leans to it, turn his head to the wall and not away from it.'

Captain Louis Nolan, 1852

News from a California local newspaper: 'From trash dumpers to naked men, the Tujunga Ponds Wildlife Sanctuary has attracted an array of troublemakers, frustrating police who have found it nearly impossible to catch anyone in the hostile terrain. The Sanctuary is closed to the public to protect animals such as ducks and crawdads*. Time to bring in the cavalry. Police and city officials announced that mounted patrols will spend weekends working the 13-acre site.' ['Crawdads', incidentally, are the freshwater lobster-like crustaceans also known as crawfish.]

'*Rhythm and Balance Established in All Paces*' – Merlin's report said, 'Very stiff to the left.'

Jo Sullivan: 'There can be all sorts of reasons for this. Long term, it might be a simple matter of having a favoured side, like we tend to be left- or right-handed, and likewise, have a favoured side when we ride. As with sports players who use one hand much more than another, muscle development is different (just look at tennis player Rafael Nadal's arms), and so your horse might benefit from a bit of physio on, say, the neck muscles. There might be a tooth problem on one side. You look at all the possibilities and try to solve whatever it is before the horse goes out. A lot of extra work on the lunging rein can help, going round the other way.' When Merlin went on duty, he was no longer stiff to the left.

'*Introduced to Trot Poles and Jumps*' – not a problem for Merlin the ex-hunter, but before jumping with a rider the horses are introduced by loose-schooling them.

Jo: 'We chase them round, basically. Some of them have never seen a jump before and have no idea what to do. We're watching the way they tackle the problem, watch their footfalls, and try and get a notion of what to expect when we get on their backs. The ones like Merlin who just go for it and have no fear, we call honest jumpers. We'll have no bother getting them up to the standard, which is our highest jump of three foot nine [1m 14cm]. You want them to jump calmly, relaxed, not to look and think about it. Officers don't expect to be jumping over obstacles every day, but if they do come across a fallen tree or a telegraph pole, they have to be confident that the horse won't stop dead and throw them over the other side.'

'LEAPING, HOW TO BE PRACTISED

'The riding-school is a bad place to teach a young horse to leap. The bar, with its posts, is very apt to frighten the animal, and the use of the whip, often administered to make him go up to the bar, gives the horse a thorough aversion to it.

'Take the horses into a field and over a low fence first, or a small ditch, not backward and forward over one and the same thing to disgust them, but over what obstacles are in the way, and then to the stables.

'Few horses refuse, if led on by a steady horse, and in this, as in every other lesson, let the increase be made by degrees.

'Always leap the horse on the snaffle, and do not be in a hurry.'

Captain Louis Nolan, 1852

Stand and Move Correctly to Open/Shut School Doors' – like the farmers of old, doing their rounds on their Galloway ponies and expecting to be able to open gates with their sticks without dismounting, so the police horse must learn to stand by a gate while his rider flicks open the catch, go through, and move correctly so it can be closed. This test created some special interest around the yard, as Merlin was already well known for having a particular affinity with locks and latches, bolts and catches, and for puzzling out how to beat them. With Merlin's abilities already proven in opening doors he shouldn't, this was an important discipline. There will be occasions on duty when the horse has to be led, perhaps through narrow passageways, through gates, even into buildings, and his rider must be confident that he's seen it all before.

'Mounted from Ground' – there are mounting blocks at the school and the police stations, but the situation is bound to arise when a dismounted officer needs to get back on without any steps up, and perhaps in a hurry too.

Jo Sullivan: 'Again, not normally a problem, but we did have a horse here a few years ago that just would not allow his rider to get on from the ground; he would not have it at all. Fine with the blocks, absolutely no go any other way. Well, we can't accept that. Maybe an officer might be able to find a bench or a low wall, but you could have been forced off your horse in a riot, or something happens while you're dismounted that needs urgent action. You can't be roaming around the street, looking for a leg up.'

Mounting from the ground puts an extra strain on the horse, and more so when the rider is in full riot kit. Horses will go to a Public Order Day, when the officers are wearing the lot – and very heavy some of them are – and mounting is done from the ground. The officers commanding must be sure that this can happen; if it doesn't, it's back to training school.

'If any of the horses will not allow the men to mount, put a cavesson [special nose-band] on, stand in front of the horse, raise the line with the right hand, and play with it, speaking to the horse at the same time to engage his attention, whilst the man quietly mounts. No one else should be allowed near, as the more people round a horse the more alarmed he is, and the more difficult to manage. As soon as the man has mounted, turn your back to the horse and walk on, leading him round with the other horses – he will soon follow their example. A few dismounted men are necessary to take hold and lead those horses that are unsteady when mounted, and if any one of them stands still, take care that the man trying to lead him on does not pull at his bridle, and look him in the face, which will effectually prevent the animal from moving forward. Make the man who leads the horse turn his back and go on, and, in almost every case, the horse will follow.'

Captain Louis Nolan, 1852

Along with accepting all nuisances, mounting from the ground was Merlin's earliest pass mark on his Amber programme. Dealing with enquiries was another. The full title is '*Stand Calmly to Deal with Public Enquiries.*' It can be quite testing and, of course, cannot be tested in the classroom. Out in the street, the member of the public might be running up, waving a map – 'Excuse me, officer, can you tell me where such-and-such is' – and the horse looks and thinks, what on earth is that? The enquirer might well want to stroke the horse and ask if he'd like a Sharps' Extra-strong (Polo is the mint of choice at Imber Court). In London's busy thoroughfares, there will be dozens of these little incidents every day, mostly concerning people who don't know anything at all about horses and who won't appreciate that a copy of the *London A–Z* may represent a threat – or, in Merlin's case, something to eat.

The Houston Police Department Mounted Patrol has around 40 horses representing many different breeds, some of which are Percheron, Belgium, Quarter Horse,

Hanoverian, Tennessee Walker, Dutch Warmblood, Thoroughbred and Spotted Saddle Horse. Geldings and mares are acceptable, minimum height of 15.2 hands, between the ages of two and fifteen years.

A new horse will be assessed at the Mounted Facility and put through such obstacles as tarpaulins, fireworks and smoke. Also, the horse will be assessed while working alone and in groups with other Mounted horses. Harassment and crowd control situations will be introduced at this point. Next, the horse and trainer will move outside the Mounted Facility to the major parks and Houston Intercontinental Airport. After successful completion of these initial training phases the horse will be exposed to the central business district. This downtown geographical area is very dynamic for training as there are major construction projects ongoing, continuous vehicular and pedestrian traffic, water obstacles, kerbs and ever-changing terrain.

After acceptance to the Mounted Unit the horse and rider will continue equine training. As a rule, the entire Mounted Unit has training once a month. During this training there will be primarily equitation and ground training, formation, crowd control, harassment and loud noise (fireworks, sirens, etc.) exercises. Also, all mounted officers and their mounts must pass a four-week Natural Horsemanship instructional class using Pat Parelli's principles.

'*Has Been Ridden in Town Environment on Several Occasions*' and '*Trot Calmly on the Roads*' are just about getting more practice and more becoming used to the working environment.

Jo Sullivan: 'Merlin never got over his liking for handbags. We'd be walking along nicely, and he'd spot a woman by the kerb and his head would go, and suddenly he'd have a handbag in his mouth and you'd be saying sorry. Nobody minded – he didn't eat the bag. I'd just have to get it off him and, like a child with a new toy, he didn't necessarily want to give me it until he'd had his bit of fun.

'Or, he'd see some flowers growing by the roadside and that was just as sudden. One minute you're progressing peacefully; in a twinkle, you're at right angles to the road and he's eating the flowers. Or he's dived into the bushes after something he fancies and you're coming out covered in foliage, and the escort rider's laughing her head off. Oh, it's Merlin again. He'd eat anything and everything and yet, oddly enough, he didn't pinch anything out of people's shopping. There might be someone with an open basket and there'd be lettuce and tomatoes easily reachable, but he didn't go for that – maybe he knew that was a step too far.'

'*Pass or Go Away from Other Horses Confidently and Willingly.*' Says Jo: 'It's usually easier to ride a young horse out of the school on our own, trot around for an hour and come back than it is to go out in half-section [see page 44] and then, after half an hour, split up. Horses like to be together, and most of the time when they've gone to duty they will be riding in pairs. But, again for certain, the occasions will arise when one has to go off for some reason and leave the other behind. So we have to introduce that here. We start off with a walk around the block to meet up again, then two blocks, and so on.'

While it's true that, generally, any horse mate is better than no mate, there are likes and dislikes.

Jo: 'We humans probably can't understand why Horse A doesn't want to be with Horse B, or vice versa. It's easier with people – so-and-so is boring, or conceited, or always moaning, or never buys his round – but with horses it's not the why that matters. If one horse doesn't like another, we have to adjust the practicalities accordingly. We had one once that wouldn't go in half-section with any grey horse – can't explain that.

'Or, you might get a bit of bother developing as you go along. When we go out in pairs, the experienced horse always takes the outside position. Then the day comes when junior has to try the outside, and sometimes the old horse doesn't like it: he's been displaced from his rightful role as senior professional. The ears go back, he gets the grumps and tried a bit of passive resistance, non-co-operation.'

If one horse really doesn't like the other, tensions can rise and sometimes spill over. A horse can move and kick another horse in much quicker time than a rider can hope to control. They can bite, too.

Jo: 'It's rare but it does happen. It probably won't if you have one argumentative, stroppy animal and one that's laid-back and doesn't care. I suppose there must be some sort of vibe that says "Am I bothered? Not at all", so the stroppy one won't do anything. If you get two bossy, highly-strung mares together, well, you might have a spat, so you try and keep them well apart as you go along.

'And, as with people, horses can get tired and irritable after a long, hard week. They might be coming home after a good few hours out, hungry, wanting to be back in their stables. People think of old Neddy the draught horse walking up and down all day long with a plough, and doing it day after day. If that did happen, it cannot have been with a young horse because the young ones here could never take that amount of work without objecting in some way.

'Merlin was the ideal, really: he was happy on his own, he was happy in company. The slight danger with him wasn't an argument with another horse, but that the two of them would set each other off, almost as if they'd cooked up some mischief together. Opportunities for fun, that's what Merlin looked for, not opportunities for disagreement.'

There are several report headings connected with appearance and uniform. '*Issued with Full Uniform Kit*', which includes the regulation bit, and '*Accepts Quarter Sheet and Long Riding Mac*'.

Full Uniform Kit – the main change here is from the light snaffle and single rein to the much heavier, police-duty bridle-bit with double reins. This is much less of a problem than it used to be, with the old, no-compromise like-it-or-not bit. Now, so long as it looks well and uniform from the outside, individual preferences can be accommodated on the inside. Even so, reins and bit must be strong and built for business. If the horse, for whatever reason, doesn't want to stop or turn, he must have the matter brought clearly to his attention.

The third aspect of horse-uniform is '*Accepts Spurs Without Complaint*'. These are not like some of the fiercer cavalry spurs, which have sharp points or other energising, skin-pricking devices like toothed wheels – rowels – that would look more at home on a giant can-opener. Nor must the horses and riders earn their spurs by riding into battle for the first time or being dubbed 'Sir Merlin'. The police spur is a very unglamorous bit of blunt metal strapped to the boot, used as much for direction changing and teamwork – in sideways movement, for instance – as for increasing forward speed.

Jo Sullivan: 'There are a few, rare exceptions but generally police officers do not carry whips. They don't use whips, and they can't be seen to be using whips – it all has to be with hands and legs and, when the situation demands it, spurs. They're just another thing to introduce and for the horse to get used to. We'll bring them in after maybe three or four months, and the first time with some horses it's "Wahey, what's this, what are you doing?", while others take no notice at all. In the end, they all realise it's a simple signal: to go this way or that.'

'The Spur has till now only been used to inflict punishment when a horse refused to obey the pressure of the leg, or to oblige him to go up to an object he was shy of. It was not considered as an "aid", but only a means of punishment. It is, on the contrary, the most powerful agent we have, without which it would be impossible to break in a horse perfectly. Those horses that are hot-tempered, vicious, or of great mettle; whose temper disposes them to break from the restraint of the bit in spite of the strongest arm, can only be reduced to obedience by the gradual and judicious use of the spur. With the spur, of course combined with the assistance of a good hand, you can perfect the education of the most intractable, and infuse spirit into the most sluggish animals. At the same time, it requires great prudence, and a thorough knowledge of the horse, to use the spur so as to obtain the proper results.

'The object is to unite the horse's powers at the centre of gravity, that is, between the forehand and haunches; and it is by the combined use of hand and leg that we attain this.

'But suppose, when you stick the spurs into him, he throws up his head, and dashes off with you? This could not happen to me because I should never communicate an impulse with the leg, which I could not control with the hand. I begin by touching his sides so lightly, and taking it so coolly, neither moving hand nor leg, that the horse is never alarmed, thinks nothing of it at first, and thus I go on, gradually increasing the dose till he takes as much as is "necessary", and "cannot help himself".

'We have already the power of keeping the horse on the straight line, which is indispensable to bring the use of the spur into play; for had we not this power, on the first application of the spur, the horse, instead of raising his forehand and bringing his haunches under him, thus concentrating his strength, would turn his haunches in or out, and avoid the necessity of bringing them under him.

'But what is of still greater importance is that judgment and knowledge of the horse's temper, which will at all times prevent our communicating an impulse to the horse, with the spur is stronger than what we can easily control with the hand.

'Suppose your horse at a walk bearing the weight of five pounds on your bridle-hand; when you close your legs to him, you will feel the effect of the impulse communicated in the additional weight thrown on your hand and this weight augments in proportion to the impulse given. On feeling this additional weight on the bridle-hand, do not give way to it but keep the bit-hand low and steady, and play with the right snaffle-rein; the horse, finding the bit an insurmountable obstacle, will by degrees learn, instead of throwing his weight forward when the impulse is given by the leg, to throw it back, and bring his haunches under him; but should you, instead of closing the leg gently to him the first time, put both spurs into his sides, the horse would throw so much weight forward from the great impulse received that he would probably pull the reins out of your hands; your object would thus be defeated in the beginning and the horse, having burst from your control on the first application of the spur, by throwing his weight forward, would ever after try to do the same.

'The spur must therefore be applied with caution and delicacy.

'The rider, by closing his legs to the horse, brings the rowels quite close to his sides so that on the word "Spur" (given in a quiet voice), he merely touches his horse's sides, retaining at the same time a steady feeling of the bit reins so as to present all opposition equal to the impulse communicated by the spur. Then make much of the horses and quiet them, taking care to square them, should they have stepped to either side with their hind-legs.

'When the spur is applied on the move, halt them to quiet them.

'You increase by degrees the use of the spur until the horse will stand its application without throwing any weight on the hand, without increasing his pace or without moving, if applied when standing still.

'If the horse kicks at the spur, it is a sign that his weight is too much forward; if he rises or capers, his weight is too much on the haunches. The rider's mind must therefore be directed to keeping the weight between the two, and when it is there his horse is properly balanced. This lesson, if well carried out, has a moral effect on the horse, which accelerates its results.

'If the impulse given by the leg or spur is always controlled by the hand, the pain the animal suffers is at all times in proportion to the resistance he offers; his instinct will soon teach him that he can diminish and even avoid it by yielding at once to what is required of him; he will not only submit, but soon anticipate our wishes.'

Captain Louis Nolan, 1852

Everybody has seen the films where the cowboy digs in his spurs and sets off across the prairie in a cloud of dust. In police work, spurs are much more likely to be a gentle reminder: you are meant to be taking me slowly forward here, not standing still or backing off. Prairies do come into the job, however, or the Surrey equivalent. If a horse were to be schooled only in the indoor arenas, on the streets and in the towns, no one could vouch for the effect of going on duty and suddenly one morning seeing Hampstead Heath or Hyde Park. *Works in Open Spaces and Woodland Areas*' is at the top of the Green report on training.

Jo Sullivan: 'We have to pre-empt any kind of crazy behaviour, so we take them out into the fields and along bridleways, give them a good canter in the countryside, as far as we can around here. We'll start off on the old showground and move on to the 40 acres we have at the back, and more open places, and mix it with roadwork. They have to understand that the freewheeling and the disciplined patrolling are all part of the same job. You can take some horses out on a canter in the wilds of Surrey, and then back on the road and they're all buzzed up because they've been cantering. We have to make sure here that the horses are used to change, and can adapt.'

The Queensland Mounted Police Unit was founded in 1846, 13 years before Queensland became independent from the Colony of New South Wales. The horse was king in this wide and rugged terrain, equally important to citizens and police in town and country, but by the 1920s there was a new king: the motorcar. Over time, the Mounted Unit was cut to mostly ceremonial duties.

This mistake was not fully realised until the 1980s, when the ideas and policies of having Mounted Police were re-adopted with new enthusiasm. Based in Brisbane, the Unit now has 18 horses on active duty, for crowd management, mounted searches, operational patrols and whatever else comes along. All the horses are former racers, for speed and agility.

While the strength of the Mounted arm appears to be declining in UK constabularies, elsewhere in the world there is more optimism. The Police Mounted Division of Sri Lanka was established in 1921, when the island, then called Ceylon, was under British rule. In 1948, police equestrian activities were reorganised and expanded, with local Sri Lankan recruits coming in for the first time, and another reorganisation of 1956 gave the Division one inspector, two sergeants, 22 constables and 23 thoroughbred horses imported from Australia.

Numbers have been increased since then, and new

stables set up. In 1998, the French warmblood breed Selle Français was introduced, a type used in Europe for show jumping and eventing, which generally stands over 16 hands. These horses, said the Sri Lankan police, were 'in keeping with international standards because of their majestic appearance and calmness'. At the last count there were 36 horses on the roster of this growing unit, plus 10 officers, 14 sergeants and 38 constables.

'*Perform Basic Lateral Movements*' – by this time the young horses know that pressure from the right leg means move to the right, while left leg means move to the left, which is something that doesn't necessarily come naturally. It's a question of understanding what the rider is looking for. The horses usually want to please but sometimes need a light reminder from the schooling whip to learn left from his right. When that's clear, they move on to sideways movements that don't at all come naturally in a group of other horses, and with the legs crossing and uncrossing, which are quite intricate matters to train. This is all very necessary; you never know what's going to happen at a football match or in another, less amenable kind of big crowd, and the officer must be confident that the trained horse is one that can move in any and all directions, when asked to do so.

'*Ridden in Ride, Introduced to Low Level of Troop Drill*' – in the early remount rides, the horses learn the basics of troop drill – walk and trot around in various manoeuvres in pairs and fours. They build up to the same figures at a canter, training instant response to team requirements in a confined space.

Jo Sullivan: 'When they're out there in the middle of a riot, there'll be a senior officer calling commands to pairs, fours, eights, and there can't be any delay in responding. Like soldiers, they can't stand there arguing or wondering what to do next.'

Some of the thresholds for passing the course – *'Accept Uniform Bit Without Evasion'* and *'Successfully Ridden by Other Members of Staff'* – are obvious enough but still have to be proved. As training neared its end, Merlin's other members of staff included PC Karen Howell, by then designated as his probable handler and partner. Unlike most blind dates, this one lasted a fortnight and neither party had the option of feigning an appointment elsewhere, receiving a planned mobile phone interruption or nipping off to the loo and doing a runner. Certainly there was the possibility of horse and officer not agreeing to become engaged, but with a horse like Merlin and an officer like Karen such a disaster was thought most unlikely (see pages 90–1).

'Patrolling up to Two Hours Daily' – this is an endurance matter, and a test of physical fitness. Horses need to be able to cope with two hours easily before going to duty can be contemplated. These are young horses and, like human children, not yet up to the rigours of long-distance running. When commissioned into full-time policing, patrols will remain around the two-hour mark for a while, but three and four hours will be coming up, and the football can be nine, ten, eleven hours.

There are several elements to this. One is the weight being carried; a large male officer in full kit is quite a load. There is also the mental element in a young horse, where everything he meets is new. With more experience, new things become old hat and so don't affect the mental state so much.

Jo: 'If you're riding around for two hours, you might come across a bus queue, with shopping bags and parcels, mothers with children and buggies. Left to himself Merlin would be there until the bus came so he has to learn that all these very interesting things are not his concern. We could see a building site, say, for the first time, and it might take us a good five minutes to get past it. Everything's going on. The horse is looking, taking it in, maybe reacting badly to the noise, maybe once you're past there's another different noise behind that the horse wants to know about. This is all tiring. He's looking, learning and, like any student, can't do too much for too long or it becomes counter-productive.

'So, you're past the building site, and you walk along nicely, when suddenly school's out and all these kids are charging about and yelling. If you do that every day for two hours to a young horse fresh from the fields in Ireland, one day he'll look at you and the message will be there: "Sorry, I can't do it any more." You can ruin a good horse that way. You have got to be very, very careful about when and how much you push a young horse to do more work. Softly, softly, that's the way to do it.'

From *The Times of India*:

The Mysore Police Department Mounted Company Commandant, S G Maribashetty, led the Dasara procession successfully for a record period of 35 years but he was due to retire on September 30 2013, five days before the Dasara celebrations commenced. The city police wrote to the government to seek an extension of Maribashetty's service by one month because of his experience and talent in leading the procession, meanwhile training D C P Prabhashankar of the

City Armed Reserve for the job in case the government did not agree.

Maribashetty first led the Dasara procession in 1976 and has done so in different ranks as sub-inspector, inspector, deputy superintendent of police, and additional superintendent of police (Commandant). The Dasara procession and the Torchlight Parade were suspended only on two occasions since 1976 when the State was hit by plague and drought.

The procession leader has to take command from the chief minister at Mysore Palace, by saluting the state deity Chamundeshwari, which is taken on a lead elephant. The procession of tableaux by cultural troupes then proceeds to the Bannimantapa Parade grounds, 5km away.

In the evening, the leader opens the Torch Light Parade after taking command from the governor at the parade grounds, where the Mounted Company exhibit their skills in equestrian sports. The event is attended by over 40,000 people.

Maribashetty is a native of Badami (Bagalkot district). He developed his interest in horse riding when he was a child after seeing the students of Sainik School in Bijapur riding horses. After joining the police department he got an opportunity. Maribashetty has won laurels at various national and international equestrian sports. In 1997, he met with a road accident in Andhra Pradesh and his leg was fractured, but this didn't prevent him from leading the procession the same year.

The mental work doesn't stop once the horse is back in the stable. We don't understand exactly what goes on in a horse's mind, just as we don't really know what our pet dog is dreaming about when we say he's chasing rabbits, but there is no doubt that the day's patrol has to be processed in some way by the young horse. If it were not so, the horse would be untrainable. Every time he saw a motorbike it would be the first motorbike he'd ever seen. Or heard.

After every walkabout, pictures and sounds are somehow recorded in the memory bank and classified.

Jo Sullivan: 'Quite how a horse files things under "No problem", "Not sure" or "Don't like it", we can never hope to understand, but we do have to understand that it happens and make our progress in the training accordingly.'

We can't call it thinking but it's the equine equivalent and surely just as tiring.

Jo: 'He [the horse] doesn't turn round and say, "That's enough, I'm going home." You have to say that for him. A tired horse will start tripping up, falling over its feet, or reacting to things he wouldn't normally react to, shaking his head – you don't have to be a great psychologist to spot it. You know, and so you take a little step back in the schedule, and you think about it and work something out, and try not to make the same mistake again.'

And so, eventually, with great patience and meticulous attention to the detail of a horse's experience, a two-hour patrol, even out of Great Scotland Yard, is all in a day's work.

Jo: 'Merlin was – is – a very inquisitive animal. He wants to be into everything. The result of that in his early days was that he found street work very tiring. He couldn't walk down the road and ignore things; he had to look and find out, and that was very exhausting for him. He was one of the ones that took longer to get up to the two-hour mark, just because he was so curious about every little thing he saw.'

'*Inside or Outside of Half-Section*' – Merlin had no difficulty with this until he realised that outside was the senior position, the one where the boss horse went, and so he always fancied that – except, of course, inside gave more opportunities for flower-eating and handbag-snatching.

'*Able to Stand and Move Accordingly to Deal with Moving Traffic*' – trainers are not police officers and so have no powers to stop and direct traffic. What they can do is stand the horse at road junctions to watch the world go by at high speed and, when the horse is used to that, stand in the middle of it all – the busier the junction, the better.

Jo: 'We start with a quiet junction, of course, and build up gradually. When we make that move right into the traffic, with cars and everything else going every which way, the first problem usually is that the horse doesn't like traffic on his inside – he's accustomed to being passed on his outside, when he's going along the road, so when you move to the centre of the road to turn right, here are the cars and buses where they've never been before. A lot of horses react to that, so standing in the filter lane is actually the point of it, not the right turn. If there is a reaction you stand, let the horse have a good look, let him process the experience, then move on. The last thing you want on that first occasion is a skip lorry coming up on your inside, with chains rattling and black smoke pouring out. Even worse if it goes over a bump.'

A lot of planning has to go into this. Routes and timing are part of the gradual process, and it must be done with minimum effect on the motoring public who, generally, are very considerate.

Jo continues: 'Roundabouts are good, traffic coming in and out in all directions. Quite a few motorists never quite master roundabouts, but we have to. Even with the planning, the traffic in Thames Ditton is not in on it, so we have to be willing to experiment and extemporise as we see things, and all without putting the horse or any driver in danger.'

After more and more practice, the horse comes to regard modern traffic as just another circumstance of his new world but, no matter how many skip wagons, boy racers and 40-ton artics have gone past on his inside without a reaction, there will always be something new when Merlin goes on duty.

Jo: 'But the reaction then has to be a controlled reaction. I'll give you an example – I was riding a horse near the end of his training, just walking along on a busy dual carriageway, and we were coming up to a service station. I didn't realise but they were demolishing part of it and, as we came up, there was a crane with a wrecking ball, smashing the top off the roof, with a huge bang, a great cloud of dust and all the noise of falling bits of building. If that had happened when he'd just started, my horse would very probably have reared up, turned and run. As it was, he raised his head, stopped, looked, and after a minute or two was ready to walk on. That's what you want. Life is full of surprises but the horse learns, and has enough trust in his rider to realise that none of it is worth making a fuss about.'

'*Confident and Safe to Ride Out Alone.*' Comment: 'Cries a lot but does not misbehave.' On his early solo rides, Merlin would start whinnying and neighing the minute he was outside the gate. He was missing his friends but unlike some horses, he didn't take matters any further and start being naughty.

Jo: 'He wouldn't do anything wrong, which is why I put that comment because some horses get more distressed and play up quite a lot. But he did whinny and sing all the way round, and when you leave the school and he does that, the other horses in the stables can hear him and they start up a chorus. The environment they're in here, always riding in pairs, means that the solo trip comes as a bit of a shock – "What's going on, where's my pal? This is new, this isn't what we do".

'As well as being alone, there's the silence. No chatter from the two riders, so I chatted to Merlin. He never took that extra step and messed about, but I had to stop the crying, which is done with the voice: you say things in soothing tones. I used to sing nursery rhymes to Merlin and give him a pat and tell him that everything was all right. He'd quieten down, and when I stopped singing and wittering on, he'd start up again. I never tried any other sorts of rhymes – I think maybe Merlin would have liked rap but I'm no good at that. Anyway, like everything else, he got used to the solo riding, stopped his crying and went on to be a star.'

'If the show of force accompanied by a dispersal order does not result in a voluntary dispersal, the most effective yet least dangerous instrument of dispersal is the police horse.'

San Jose (California) Police Department
Mounted Unit Training Manual

Law enforcement may be a subculture that thrives on conformity, but the San Jose Police Department Mounted Unit is a model of diversity, from Larry Holmes with his handlebar moustache to Sergeant Urban, whose long blond hair and manicured red fingernails hardly fit the stereotype of a police sergeant. Married to a fellow cop and mother to three small children, the buoyant 34-year-old Urban has 11 years of law enforcement experience behind her, including a three-year stint as a sniper in MERGE, the department's SWAT team.

The uniform includes riding breeches with blue-and-gold stripes, black riding boots and navy-blue campaign hats, with a badge of crossed cavalry sabres on their lapels. 'That's what makes mounted officers,' Urban said. 'They have to earn it.'

San Jose has had Mounted Police in one capacity or another since 1911; the unit presently has 12 horses on active duty, two in training, 11 mounted officers, two sergeants and a civilian trainer.

With increased emphasis on community policing, Mounted Police in America have become more common. A smartly uniformed officer astride a beautiful horse cannot be bettered for creating a positive image, and helps break police–citizen barriers.

Fellow officers on foot may look at their Mounted colleagues as the public-relations police, just standing around and looking good. 'Let me tell you,' says Sergeant Urban, 'those same officers are the first to say, "Oh, thank goodness you were here in front of us, protecting us and moving that crowd back."'

'*Horse Ridden after Dark*' – here, the concern is not so much the darkness but the lights – street lights, moving lights, flashing lights, and the shadows they cast, all potential causes of fear and spooking. Merlin, by now seemingly immune to anything his trainers could show him, could not see a problem in the dark.

'*Has Attended MPSTC Level 3*' – the Metropolitan Police Specialist Training Centre at Gravesend, Kent is a fairly new facility, where police hold firearms, public order and other special training, with 'film set' mock-ups of a mini-town, football ground, bank, shops and so on. Public order is about maintaining the peace so that everyone can exercise his/her right to go about their lawful business, and this includes those who gather to march or demonstrate, as well as those who wish to carry on regardless. Every Met officer, and every Met horse, goes through the basic Level 3 course as a part of qualifying for the job. The horses will go back, again and again, to reach the Advanced Level 1, but that was some way ahead for Merlin.

Jo Sullivan: 'Gravesend is where we practise with mock riots. We see what the horses are like with fire and smoke, lots of noise and people charging about everywhere, banging on riot shields. Merlin loved it. I gave him "*Excellent in all aspects of the day*", and so he was.'

Report from an American police officer: 'Two Mounted Units were in the district patrolling a high crime area. The mounted officers got into a fight with a group of bad guys, and the assist call came over the radio. I was still three blocks away [in a patrol car] when the assist was called off, and I saw something moving toward me from a darkened street – a riderless police horse. He made a left turn and galloped northbound on the one-way southbound thoroughfare, on a long stretch without crossings where speeds of 50mph are common.

'I swung in behind him, and turned on every light I had to silhouette the horse so that southbound drivers couldn't miss such an unusual sight. It worked better than I'd hoped as southbound traffic moved to both kerbs and stopped. A few blocks ahead was a major intersection, and just as I'd determined to risk passing the horse and race to the intersection to stop all traffic, the horse stopped galloping and turned toward the sidewalk. He walked slowly onto the sidewalk, stopped, and pressed his nose against a house wall. Now came the hard part. I got out of my car and walked toward the horse with no idea of how he might react.

'I had a pretty big audience by this time, and it would have been terribly embarrassing if the horse decided to continue his odyssey. I moved slowly as I reached out and put my hand around his halter. Seconds later I was petting his head and talking dumb stuff to him, just like I do with my dogs. The best part came when the mounted officer arrived to retrieve his horse. His gratitude was dwarfed only by his obvious affection for his horse, and his relief that no harm had come.'

'*Kingston on more than One Occasion*' – The Royal Borough of Kingston upon Thames, scene of Saxon coronations, is one of the busiest shopping centres in Greater London. It's the equivalent in retail trade of Covent Garden and, as the former-market-turned-tourist-trap will be on the beat for Imber Court horses based at Great Scotland Yard, very useful in lots of ways. For a start, it's within riding distance from the training centre, and the level of traffic is roughly on a par with London. If a horse can deal with Kingston, he can handle anything.

Jo Sullivan: 'We take them there near the end of their

training. It is, for a young horse, a tremendous experience, but first we go to Surbiton – similar, and nearer, but not anything like as busy. Once we've done a couple of Surbitons, we can then think about the big city.

'It takes 45 minutes to an hour to get there, along major roads, so we have to have built up to cope with two and three hours of road-work. Merlin was very good in traffic, so getting there was no problem. He likes people – he's a real people-horse – and Kingston centre, the market square, is full of people, and they don't see horses very often. Whenever we go there, we are mobbed, so when I went with Merlin, he could not have been more pleased. And not just because of the attention he was getting.

'I have certain places I like to go – for instance, where we can see the automatic fountain shooting out of the ground – but the highlight is my spot right next to one of the fruit and veg stalls. The stallholder always gives my horse a couple of carrots, which Merlin thought was great, and then people come up and ask what does he like? Carrots and apples are generally the best choice although Merlin would eat anything – bananas, anything.

'As I say, it is a wonderful experience, especially on the mental side. I've ridden Merlin there in heavy traffic, negotiated the one-way system, and now we're standing, people-watching, getting treats, in a pedestrian area, no cars, and he can relax his mind for 20 minutes. If he lifts his tail, someone will dive out and clear it up – happiness all around. But I have to bear in mind the journey home, so we can't stay too long. We have to get back into the one-way system and along the main roads, and back to the stables, tired but pleased with life.'

'*Horse Ridden with Public Order Kit*' – this includes the leg guards and the visor, strange objects, but it's just about the last thing they have to put up with and horses very seldom object. Merlin didn't, nor did he realise that with 'Patrol Saddle Issued', he was ready to go on duty.

Horse-mounted police patrols in the United States are often traced back to the Texas Rangers. The Rangers were formally organised in 1835 as a quasi-military force to patrol the frontiers between the Colorado and Trinity rivers, and to protect the Texas frontier from Indian attacks. Following the Civil War, they began to concentrate on standard police work against outlaws. Other states – for example, Arizona and New Mexico – also began horse patrols to reduce predations by outlaws.

Manchester is the largest city in the state of New Hampshire, with a population of 110,000. The police department inaugurated a Mounted Unit in 1999, with a federal grant to enhance community policing, after reviewing the positive impact such units had had elsewhere. Budgetary cuts in 2004 almost forced closure of the Unit but it was saved through the help of sponsors and donors.

Although very small – only two horses and three officers – the Unit fulfils all the roles expected of Mounted Police. Horse recruitment policy is for gelding Percheron or draught horses between the ages of five and twelve years old, sorrel or black in colour, at least 16 hands high, but because the most important qualifications are the horse's aptitude and disposition, exceptions may be made. Police horses must be able to work without difficulty in a busy, noisy urban environment, should be brave and obedient, and able to cope with confrontational situations without becoming agitated or upset.

Chapter Four

Merlin of The Yard

In July 2011, a public family picnic was being held on the Toronto Exhibition grounds and trips were offered to the guests on a cart pulled by two Clydesdale horses. During one such trip, the horses saw something that made them bolt and the driver and his three passengers were thrown from the cart.

As the Clydesdales headed at full speed towards the crowd of picnickers, pulling the empty cart, Constables Broske and Van Overbeek of the Toronto Police Service Mounted Unit were returning to the nearby stables. The two officers immediately galloped over and stood their police horses nose to nose across the road, in the way of the Clydesdales, in an attempt to stop them. The tactic had no effect, so the officers had no choice but to get out of the way and give chase.

Constable Van Overbeek overtook the cart and

manoeuvred her horse in front of the Clydesdales, which did then begin to slow their pace. Constable Broske rode his horse beside the charging heavyweights, keeping them in a straight line along the road and away from the excited spectators by the roadside. As the caravan slowed, other police officers were able to jump on to the empty cart and bring the horses under control.

More usually, it's outside the nightclubs that the horses see the most action in Toronto. Half a dozen mounted officers patrol at weekends in the entertainment district, dispersing crowds and breaking up fights.

'You walk into a situation on foot where fists are flying and you usually get a few yourself,' explained Staff Sergeant Patterson. 'When you move a horse in between them, it stops right away.'

The word 'constable' comes from Count of the Stable, who was the chief officer of the medieval nobleman's household when horses were the prime asset up at the castle. By the 16th century the meaning of the term had developed to 'Officer of the Peace', and later the parish constable was the appointed Conservator of the Peace in his district or township. When organised police forces came in, that office of constable was incorporated into the duties and authority of the Force members.

Mounted officers are police officers first and always, regardless of horse. They hold the office of Constable, they have the powers and responsibilities, and they just happen to be on a horse. Admittedly, Mounted Police can do things that those on foot cannot do, but it works the other way too.

PC Karen Howell: 'At the extreme, it can be embarrassing. I stopped somebody in a car who had a baby in the back seat who wasn't strapped in – that's a fixed penalty offence these days. I was on my own with Merlin, so I asked the driver to step out of the car and then I had to write out the ticket. There was a grass verge where we were. Merlin fancied that, and when I stopped him trying to eat it, he decided he liked the look of the wing mirror as a mid-morning snack. It was impossible to write the ticket at the same time as all that, so I got off, handed the reins to the offending driver, checked that the seat belt was in working order, and issued the £60 notice. Good old Merlin.'

Dalian city (Lüda) in Liaoning Province (People's Republic of China) opened the Mounted Policewomen's training facility to visitors after it became widely known that tourists were keen to be photographed with the policewomen on horseback.

The facility charges 50 yuan [£5.00 at today's rates] per person. The ticket includes equestrian performances, while visitors can pay additional fees to ride a horse. *China Business News* estimated the training facility has earned at least 30 million yuan in 12 years from ticket sales, which it said was a violation of regulations banning police from being engaged in activities for profit.

It was not known how the money was spent – the unit is funded by the local public security bureau. *China Business News* said the bureau allocates 3 million yuan annually to take care of the Unit's horses, plus additional funds to pay the policewomen in the unit. In 1999, the Dalian government spent 5 million yuan to build the training facility and Hong Kong Jockey Club donated 100 retired racehorses.

A Beijing lawyer was cited as saying a tax stamp cannot be found on the tickets, implying they were printed without authorisation.

Once dubbed part of the Dalian landscape, mounted policewomen are attracting more public criticism after Zhao Ming, a retired cop, described them as 'decoration'. Public security authorities lack funds and policemen while the government continues to spend large amounts of taxpayers' money on horses, Zhao added. He suggested the authorities disband the division because they could serve the city better if they worked under the tourism bureau.

The Mounted Policewomen Unit of the DPSB Patrolmen Division has 65 mounted policewomen, 100 horses, 23 motorcycles, four trailers for horse transportation, four office cars and one truck.

There was a similar sort of incident in Camden, north London. A mounted PC and sergeant had stopped to chat with people sitting at outside tables of a restaurant when a radio message came through. A 999 call had been made from that same restaurant: there was trouble inside and an arrest to be made. The sergeant passed his horse's reins to the PC and went in. Wanting to help, the PC spotted a responsible-looking security guard and asked him to hold the horses.

With the suspect handcuffed, the PC went out to call for transport only to find the horses – and the security guard – gone. There were horseshoe scratches on the ground. In sleuth mode, the PC followed the marks and met someone coming the other way, leading one horse while the other followed behind. Both were in place outside the restaurant before the sergeant came out.

Police riders also must progress, starting off on an older, experienced horse before being judged capable of taking on a lively, new, enthusiastic (maybe over-enthusiastic) horse like Merlin. Karen, when new to the job, had been given an experienced horse. After a few years, the rider was the experienced one and able to take on novices fresh out of the Imber Court stables; her second such horse was Merlin.

There is an unwritten selection procedure that goes both ways: horse for rider, rider for horse, which extends beyond experience alone. There has to be a bond between the partners, mutual respect, and you must get along with each other, as in any partnership. All horses have their own characters, and if a long-term relationship is to flower, horse and rider must be compatible.

Karen Howell: 'I don't know why they picked me for Merlin – maybe they thought I had a good sense of humour. I'd like to put it down to my inexhaustible patience. Merlin was full of energy, full of life, full-on, and he had to have some fun mixed in with the serious work.'

Merlin, the trainers decided, was definitely a potential city-centre horse but he needed a sympathetic, tolerant, persevering handler – as they all do, of course, but perhaps Merlin required a little more sympathy and tolerance. If he was smarter than your average horse, he might also be more of a challenge.

'We had a horse called Star, and every new officer who came into the Mounted Branch was given Star as his first partner. The new officer would never ask why Star had no regular partner, because he didn't know that was the case. He soon found out, though: Star's favourite trick was to wait until he'd been groomed, and then roll in some manure. If there wasn't any there, he'd make some! If being smelly wasn't bad enough, he was also afraid of large lorries. I think we just kept him so he could give our lieutenant a good laugh.'

Mounted officer, USA

In 1816 George Vaughan, a member of the Bow Street Horse Patrol, forerunners of the Met Mounted Branch, was sentenced to five years' hard labour for setting up five men for a burglary in Hoxton. He arrested them in the act for a reward of £40 per man.

The hand-over from school to duty started in February 2010 with two weeks around the stables and the local town, Thames Ditton. Karen rode Merlin, while his trainer, Jo Sullivan, rode the escort. As Karen and Merlin got to know each other, Jo recounted all the tales of escapes, handbags, flowers, blanket tricks and so on.

As Rodgers and Hammerstein put it in their musical, *The King and I*: 'It's a very ancient saying, but a true and honest thought, that if you become a teacher, by your pupils you'll be taught.' And the chorus goes, 'Getting to know you, getting to know all about you. Getting to like you, getting to hope you like me.' Very apt, don't you think, Karen?

Karen Howell: 'You could say it was love at first sight, at least for me. I'd popped in to visit him after I knew I was going to get him, and the more I saw him, the more I liked him. He is such a nice horse, and he enjoys life. Every day, it's "Hey,

90

what are we up to today? Wow, this is brilliant, let's be away, where are we going?" Some horses do the job because they're trained to, Merlin does it because he really loves it. He makes everything such a pleasure. He's a people horse – he wants to be out, a-doing. Which is why he can be a bit naughty if he's cooped up in the stable. He gets bored, and won't accept boredom and doing nothing as a reasonable situation.

'We tried him with one of those plastic balls with treats inside – hours and hours of harmless fun, indestructible. The horse is supposed to knock and nudge the ball around and gradually the treats drop out. Well, Merlin wasn't falling for that one. "Why would I nurdle and knock-about getting one treat at a time, when I can chew the top right off and get all the treats at once?"'

It's that bold spirit that makes him such a great police horse, but it also causes problems. The normal hand-over from trainer to rider is two weeks. Merlin and Karen had to have an extra week.

Karen: 'He was arguing with me, in the school. He wouldn't put his head down for me – this is important because it's part of the horse-rider profile. He has to carry my weight properly, so it's correct for his body and his muscles, and his head has to be down. So he was tossing his head about, then Jo would get on him and he'd drop his head immediately, and I would get back on him and he'd be naughty again – "No, I'm not doing that just because you say so. Jo's my friend, who are you?"'

'The balance of the horse's body and his lightness in hand depend on the proper carriage of the head and neck, and to these two points we must first and chiefly direct our attention. They should always precede and prepare the horse by their attitude for every movement about to be executed, and the rider has no power over the animal until he has rendered both these points susceptible of every impulse communicated by him. It stands to reason that if they do not lead in all turns and changes of hand, &c, &c., if in circling they are not bent to the circle, if in reining back the head is not brought home, if their carriage is not always in keeping with the different paces, the horse may execute the movements required of him or not, as he pleases, for his resources are still at his own disposal.'

Captain Louis Nolan, 1852

These were little things, and all schooling matters, though important if the working relationship was to prosper. Within the week these minor problems were resolved and off they went to Great Scotland Yard.

Merlin is a forward-going, forward-looking horse. Not yet five years old, setting out into a new, very big, very wide, very busy world, just taking everything in was exhausting enough. Initially, patrols were two hours or less but – depending on what he met and saw – Merlin could be going home tired out. He'd had a fairly easy, natural kind of a life in Ireland, then he'd lived for months in the protective, safe environment of training school – then all of a sudden there's a roundabout or a set of traffic lights. There's a lorry full of rattling scaffolding poles going past, a regimental band playing on the march, a line of 20 bikers on Harley-Davidsons, some show-off in a souped-up sports car – or, indeed, four gentlefolk in Edwardian costume, open to the elements, phut-phutting along in a De Dion Bouton – and all accompanied by a constant flow of people on every side, making noise, scurrying about their business, or wandering aimlessly, or waving their arms while shouting into mobile phones. It was enough to put any horse off his stride, and it was enough for Merlin too.

For his first week, Jo rode him and Karen escorted on an experienced horse, Monday to Thursday, and on Friday they swapped.

Karen Howell: 'We were riding past the Changing of the Guard, which was going on behind the Palace gates, and heading for Green Park, when the band struck up. Merlin did a four-footed leap in the air and threw me onto his neck, and back again when he hit the ground. I asked Jo if she was trying to fit me up with this horse, but she couldn't answer for laughing.

'Exuberant, I think, would be the word for him. He would do these leaps frequently, sometimes through sheer exuberance, mostly when he met something new or heard a noise that cut through all the other noises. A particular problem at first was meeting horses. In Hyde Park, for instance, you get a lot of civilian riders, and he'd see one of these in the distance, whinny, and jump in the air. He wanted to be with the other horses; it's natural, they are a herd animal. Fortunately, his leaps were always in a straight line so I never fell off. He's a very powerful, very athletic horse, but he responds. If I kept him going forward, and told him that I thought this was not the accepted thing to do for an animal in his position, he soon calmed down. And then it was "Who, me? Don't know what you mean".'

A new police horse was given the royal seal of approval by the Queen, naming him 'Jubilee'. The horse, with Avon and Somerset Constabulary's Mounted team, was named by Her Majesty during her visit to East Somerset as part of her Jubilee tour of the UK.

The seven-year-old bay gelding, standing at 17.3 hands, had been with the Force for three months undergoing specialist training. His rider and trainer is PC Jon Green, a Mounted section officer for 23 years.

Avon and Somerset Police Chief Constable Colin Port, who attended the naming ceremony in Ninesprings Country Park, Yeovil, said: 'We are delighted to have this unique opportunity to have one of our horses officially named by the Queen. It is an opportunity – in a small way – to be involved in celebrating Her Majesty's 60 years of public service.'

One of the worst cases of equine cruelty in the UK – or, indeed, of any kind of animal cruelty anywhere, and surely one without parallel in the horse world – came to court in 2008. Well over 100 animals – horses, donkeys and ponies – all destined for slaughter, were found in appalling conditions, some of them on the point of death through neglect, at Spindles Farm, Amersham, Buckinghamshire. Around the farm, RSPCA investigators found 32 more equines who had passed that point, left to lie in the mud where they dropped.

One of 65 survivors that came to Redwings Horse Sanctuary was six-year-old Bert. After recovering his health, he was rehomed with a South Norfolk special constable. We don't know about Bert's earlier life, but the latter part had been spent in misery and liable to end suddenly at a salami factory. Instead, Bert now became an innovative part of Norfolk Constabulary's Operation Randall, a scheme designed to combat rural crime.

A pilot project featured Bert and three more horses, handled by special constables, patrolling country areas at a country pace, providing a reassuring police presence in remote parts and gathering information on suspicious vehicles, unusual movements at night, strangers acting oddly, and generally collecting and supplying the kind of intelligence that used to find its way to the village bobby.

Merlin's debut tour of duty would be three months, with an assessment and refresher course at the end, back at Imber Court. Here is the diary entry for his first patrol, with Karen but without Jo, at the start of those three months:

'Escorted by PC Sheppard on Gryffindor. Patrol via Whitehall to Belgravia and Pimlico. Merlin stood still to deal with damaged motor vehicle. 2 hour patrol in total – no problems, horse calm throughout ride. Return to Great Scotland Yard via Whitehall.'

Gryffindor knew Karen very well. He had been her student, her first remount straight out of school; also trained by Jo Sullivan, given to her to coach into the working life. Now, five years later, Gryffindor – named after Harry Potter's house at Hogwarts – was senior horse, looking after the callow youth called Merlin.

The horses have one rest day a week, which is when Merlin felt bored and was likely to eat bits of his stable, but he was out again on Monday. The diary entry notes:

'1½ hour patrol, via Embankment, over Vauxhall Bridge, trot, back in over Blackfriars Bridge. Escorted by PC McMaster on Flintlock. No problems, horse very calm throughout ride.'

His second week was interrupted – postponed, in fact – because Merlin developed a saddle sore. The problem was resolved with a silk patch on the numnah (sheepskin pad fitted between saddle and horse's back). 'Numnah' is another cavalry word, brought home by the British Army from India.

Karen was concentrating, naturally, on Merlin's reactions to all the events that the citizens of the metropolis regard as everyday, hardly worth a look. Building works, pneumatic drills, holes in the road – these are normal and slight inconveniences to us, but big surprises to a young horse and, to Merlin, matters of great curiosity. So, would he behave himself? Would he do something embarrassing? Going by the events of his fifth outing, Merlin might have pointed out that such anxiety, however mild, was not entirely fair:

'2 hour patrol including ½ hour off horse's back. Patrol out via Pall Mall. Merlin saw rear of Buckingham Palace Guard going up Mall. Was alert but remained calm. Rode into Hyde Park, walked up Serpentine Road, escorted by PC Allen riding Zena. Went in front of PC Allen and trotted off. Behind me I could hear Zena misbehaving, which unsettled Merlin. Stopped and eventually Merlin calmed down. Unable to do any more trotting because Zena continued trying to buck and generally misbehaving. Merlin settled down and maintained his calmness even when Zena was playing up. Zena not to be used as escort in future.'

The misbehaving horse was an experienced one – a mare not known for causing trouble, but perhaps she just didn't like this young male in front of her. It was one of those horse things that we can't explain. As for Merlin, he had a ride the next day with another officer, marked 'excellent', and seemed 'a little strong' the following day with Karen, but 'settled after ten minutes'. The test was Hyde Park again, where he had clearly forgotten about his little incident, had a calm walk around and came home on the outside of his escort through Trafalgar Square:

'Very good when standing at busy junction Whitehall/ Parliament Square. Walked past a revolving cement-mixer lorry – very good with this.'

In Taipei some people questioned the appropriateness for horses to patrol the main streets that are heavily used by vehicles and motorcycles. Captain Huang Hsin-wei of the Mounted Police team said it is rather safe for people if they avoid standing behind the horses. They should also avoid holding or wielding sticks or other objects like umbrellas in front of the horses.

Those socialising in Cheltenham town centre during Race Week will see horses are not just appearing at the racecourse. Two mounted police officers will be carrying out patrols in the town centre at night, to provide additional reassurance for the large numbers visiting the festival.

Jimmy Elias, chair of Cheltenham Nightsafe, said: 'Cheltenham always has a busy night-time economy, but

Race Week is the busiest time of the year. The members of Nightsafe work hard to ensure the safety of all their customers and it is important to continue to keep it safe, so that visitors return year after year.'

The Met have some use of the indoor school at the Royal Mews, behind Buckingham Palace, and the outdoor equivalent in Hyde Park, where the Household Cavalry do their training, so Merlin could have a break from the daily rush of new experiences with a little formal schooling to remind him of his earlier lessons and increase the bond with his rider. The diary states:

> *'Rode to Royal Mews via Whitehall for lesson. Worked in school with PC Greening and Gryffindor. Merlin worked well on his own apart from when two other horses came into school and he did a huge leap towards them. He settled back down and worked quietly with six other horses. Came in via Trafalgar Square on outside.'*

Karen Howell: 'You work with the horse, listening to the messages you're getting from him. You want to introduce him to everything he's going to have to deal with, but you have to do it at a sensible pace. Obviously, you wouldn't go to a demo or the football in his first week, but you have to be equally careful with all the little events.' The diary states:

> *'2½ hour patrol, Trafalgar Square, Hyde Park, Bayswater (walk/trot). Took 10 mins to settle, tense in neck, then excellent. He was a nuisance during a stop/search – wanted to join in the search.'*

2½ hour patrol in West End/Soho. Busy patrol. Calls to robbery and an alarm. Excellent throughout, in trot and 20 mins dismounted.'

Merlin was making steady progress, perhaps better than steady, but there was still the occasional setback.

Karen Howell: 'Maybe they should have called him Zebedee, because that's what it was like sometimes: Merlin and the Magic Roundabout. One day we watched the Queen's Life Guards (QLG) go past on their horses, no reaction. The very next day, crossing The Mall after the Life Guards had just gone through, he got excited and did two big leaps. He settled down quickly enough after I rode him into St James's Park, but as we approached Buckingham Palace I saw the band at the Changing of the Guard were getting ready to leave. I trotted past, heading for Green Park, but the band started playing, and that set him off.

'He did his four-footed leaps in rapid succession. Boing, boing, boing, he wouldn't stop. We boinged through the daffodils with the other mounted officer behind us, laughing and shouting, 'Sit up straight, Karen, hold on!' and me shouting at Merlin to stop. You see lambs doing something similar when they gambol in the meadow, only this was a very strong, very athletic, 16.2 hands of a beast, weighing well over half a ton not including me, gambolling in a public park.

'I called whoa, I growled in his ear when I had the chance, and made it plain that I wasn't very happy. The message got through; he wasn't trying to upset me, he wasn't being naughty. He was a child saying, "It wasn't my fault, I didn't mean to". He was just full of the joys of spring, "spring" being the operative word. Fortunately, this was before everybody in the world had a camera-phone, or we'd have been on YouTube by tea-time.

'By the time I got him to the top of the park he was completely calm, and we rode back via Victoria Street, New Scotland Yard and Embankment without a care in the world. I did put a note in the diary that he was not to be taken to the guard changes for the time being.'

'A horse cantering on a straight line, light in hand and well balanced, is made to change leg in the same way that he is made to strike off to either hand from a walk. Violent effects of force should be avoided, which would bewilder the horse and destroy his lightness. It must be remembered that this lightness, which should precede all changes of pace and direction, and make every movement easy, graceful and inevitable, is the important condition to be sought after before everything else.

'If a horse is so far broken in, so far under control of hand and leg as to be unable to do any thing unless you wish it, all his capabilities are at your disposal; you can throw the weight on each limb in succession, and change leg, at every stride.

'The great secret is therefore this; take the weight off the legs you wish the horse to lead with. This is the only one of the many different ways laid down which is founded on principle and common sense. Try it yourself: go down on all fours, throw your weight on the left hand and leg, then try to move forward, and see whether it be not absolutely necessary to do so with the right hand and leg.'

Captain Louis Nolan, 1852

A pit bull terrier on the loose attacked a US Park Police horse in a San Francisco park, biting it in the stomach and locking onto a back leg. The horse fell and his rider was thrown to the ground. Freeing itself from its determined persecutor, the horse made for the stables at the end of the park, the pit bull in pursuit. When the dog attacked again, it had lost the advantage of surprise and received a hearty kick from the horse, which dampened its ardour somewhat.

The dog was captured and its owner arrested and charged. A spokesman said that the horse, after medical treatment, 'should recover but he was pretty chewed up'.

After five weeks, Karen judged Merlin ready for his first solo patrol. The horses have to learn to do without an escort and for the rider it's a nervous time because events cannot be predicted. Riders are police officers first, horse-teachers second, and anything that might come up has to be dealt with, which invariably means the horse having to stand still. Solo patrols are preventive policing, like the bobby on the beat, although the bobby on a horse has more visibility when sent somewhere – for example – that has been experiencing anti-social behaviour, or expected to be exceptionally busy, such as Oxford Street during the sales. A quieter route is selected for the solo introduction, not that anywhere in daytime central London can be classified as entirely quiet, not even on a Sunday.

Karen Howell: 'He couldn't have been better, really. We went down Villiers Street, Savoy Place, across The Strand into Covent Garden. He whinnied a bit, which is a question – "Where is my friend, why am I on my own?" Which is when the horse relies on his rider, to reassure, to say, "It's all right, I'm here. You do what I tell you and everything will be fine". We walked past a cement mixer and other bits and pieces by the road, and after three quarters of an hour on our own we teamed up and did an escorted hour through Lincoln's Inn Fields. No problems at all.'

Merlin was by now well settled into the daily routine. Karen arrives (after the Unit briefing), mucks out, sweeps, tidies, brings in the grooming kit, puts it on the floor, washes the horse's face, turns to look for something, and that's Merlin's moment to tip the box upside down and throw the brushes into the corner. The obvious answer would be to tie him up but Karen's view is that it's a bit of fun, no harm done, and children need to play – 'We'll just have to renew a few bits of grooming kit from time to time.' The notices on the stable door at Imber Court were repeated at Great Scotland Yard: 'Do not leave anything remotely chewable anywhere near this horse.'

Karen Howell: 'Everybody loves Dennis the Menace. There's a statue of him in the street in Dundee – that's Merlin. If Merlin was a fictional character, he'd be Just William meets Dennis the Menace. You can't get cross with him. Well, you can, but it doesn't last long.'

There's tacking up to do – the tack is cleaned every day with polish to get a good shine – and Merlin's hooves need to be oiled. Everything must look smart. The only time the oil doesn't go on is if there's a protest or a big march, where there might be fire or fireworks.

'3 hour patrol escorted by PC Lindsay-Stewart on Gawain. Rode to Chelsea and environs. Merlin generally very settled after initial 20 minutes of fizziness. Only a couple of leaps

today when he saw other horses. Stopped when shouted at and pushed on with legs. Rode to Hyde Park stables, stood still in yard for half an hour. Good on return home apart from a couple of leaps forward.'

'1½ hour patrol escorted by PC McMaster on Flintlock. Out via Villiers Street, rode up Oxford Street. Trotted round Golden Square on my own – very good when leaving escort horse. Merlin on outside on return, very calm.'

It was still early days but Merlin was doing well, for Karen and for the other officers who took him out when she was off duty. Some of the little hiccups could be expected, as the diary notes: 'Saw four horses in the park and again, once they went past, Merlin leapt forward but soon calmed down.'

'Merlin worked well in [Hyde Park] school around a cavalry horse. Became unsettled when the horse left but soon paid attention back to me. After 3½ hours out, one very tired horse.'

Tiredness is not altogether predictable and not entirely to do with the amount of legwork; how much work the horse is used to also comes into it, as in training for an athlete, but there is also the mental weariness.

Karen Howell: 'Merlin rarely gets tired these days, now he's fully experienced in everything, but initially there's a lot of learning to do. A young child can equally get tired learning its ABC or going on an exciting outing to somewhere new. Every parent knows the result – a scratchy, easily upset individual who needs to be got to bed as soon as can be. Well, it's the same with a young horse. He's had an education, sure, so he's seen traffic before and people beside him on the pavement, but there's a million and one things he hasn't seen.

'I had a young horse once that, at first anyway, couldn't take it for more than 40 minutes – all the hoo-hah and sights and sounds just exhausted him. Merlin wasn't as bad as that but there was still a lot of what you might call mental work. It is the horse equivalent of studying, learning that this happens and it's OK, and that happens, nothing to get in a state about. While he's studying, you have to monitor the amount. You watch for being fidgety, tiredness in the eyes, the walking slows down, he doesn't want to go – it's fairly obvious.

'You must never forget that inside a horse, big as he is and powerful as he is, there's a much smaller wild animal whose survival strategy is rapid flight from danger. That makes horses like Merlin all the more brave, really, because courage and standing up for himself goes right against nature.'

Police horse Tony was on duty with the Baltimore Police Department when he was shot in the line of duty. On patrol in Druid Hill Park one day, Tony's rider saw a parked car that aroused his suspicions and so moved up next to it. The driver appeared agitated and anxious to get away. As the officer leaned over to reach for the ignition key, several shots were fired from inside the car, one bullet severely wounding the officer and another hitting the horse in his hindquarters. Both victims recovered, and Tony went back on duty with the bullet still in him, the vet deciding this was better for the horse than an operation to remove it.

Four brave police horses that once worked for Greater Manchester Police are hanging up their horseshoes and retiring to The Horse Trust's sanctuary in Speen,

Buckinghamshire. Between them they have notched up nearly 50 years' service and have been involved in a wide range of duties, including public order, crowd control at football matches and city centre patrols.

Ann Firth, Groom Team Leader for Greater Manchester Police's Mounted Branch, said: 'They are big, brave horses that everyone loved riding as they knew they'd be safe. All four animals were stalwarts, and were often the first to be selected for operations as they could be used for all types of work and nothing scared them. They will be hugely missed, but everyone's thrilled that they're getting such a well-deserved retirement at The Horse Trust. After more than a decade pounding the streets of Manchester, it's lovely that they'll get to be free horses again and can spend their days grazing in the fields at the sanctuary.'

Jeanette Allen, Chief Executive Officer of The Horse Trust, said: 'We are delighted to offer Nickleby, Oliver, Fairfax and Jack lifetime sanctuary after their loyal and brave service to the police. Our staff will give them the loving care they need for the remainder of their years.'

The trust between horse and rider must run deep, because the rider will be asking the horse to do things he finds frightening, or that push his tolerance to the limits. Go up these many stone steps to clear agitators away from that massive doorway. Stand still for hours in this square while a continuous stream of people come to pat you. Walk slowly through this travelling fairground, past the dodgems and the carousels and the tipsy gang of girls shrieking with laughter while trying to give you candyfloss. Or, in one case for a Met horse, go through this narrow doorway into the relatively dark interior of a bank, and stand while I arrest this person trying to cash a forged cheque.

Among the mayhem, sights and sounds that Merlin happened across were some little spookings that could not have been foreseen. The diary notes: 'Walked across the front of the Palace when Merlin took exception to a lady in a sari and shied away.'

If he didn't like the sari, Merlin had a much bigger Asian surprise waiting for him the next week – '2½ patrol. Trafalgar Square – unsettled from start – Green Park – bolted when 50 yards away from multi-coloured elephants.'

Nothing in Merlin's training – at Imber Court, on the job, in the Royal Mews or anywhere else – could have prepared him for a series of sculptures of baby elephants (260 of them, life size, all different, mostly painted in vivid rainbow colours by famous designers and artists) that had been placed around London in the summer of 2010 to raise awareness of the species in decline in its native lands. Among the populace they caused much delight and amusement but they gave poor Merlin a severe case of the heebie-jeebies.

A horse's colour vision is roughly equivalent to that of a human with red-green colour blindness. Broadly, a horse can see blue and green, but reds, browns and yellows all look greenish, and if the lightness/darkness in shade were similar between, say, a green and a yellow, the horse could not tell them apart.

Ten minutes after the elephants, Merlin spotted two police horses in the distance and went into a jumping fit, twice, but he was learning quickly because he then walked past two more elephants without taking a blind bit of notice. Or was he in fact learning?

Whether it was their colours or not, the two elephants that Merlin walked past must have seemed somehow innocuous – but they were the only ones. He really, really didn't like the other 258, and they were scattered all over his beat, in Trafalgar Square, Parliament Square, outside Buckingham Palace. Something had to be done.

Karen Howell: 'I took him back to see them, one or two at a time, and patted him, and fed him mints, and he gradually realised that they weren't going to leap out and eat him. I can even say that eating mints with him and elephants became a pleasurable experience.'

Even if he never would trust them entirely, he came to understand that they were just a fact of life in this crazy world, to be ignored, like so many others. The diary notes: 'Very good calm ride apart from him leaping forward at a skateboarder coming at speed down the footpath.'

From time to time, Mounted Police ship out to more distant parts using a horsebox. Merlin had been in a box before but he must have forgotten about it – 'Box patrol to Richmond Park. Merlin was very excitable when I got him off the box. Two horses left before us and he did a huge leap, so I turned him on a tight circle until he calmed down.'

Days without incident were becoming more frequent – 'Excellent thoughout', 'Very responsive and calm', 'Very relaxed today sticking his nose into bins and lorries'. This was two months into his probation, and he was getting 'only leapt once today, at sudden noise from behind', 'reluctant to stop sometimes at junctions', 'good in trot although wants to go a bit too fast', 'quite heavy on my hands today' and 'Excellent coming in via Trafalgar Square which was gridlocked with motor bikes and football fans.'

'Solo patrol for 1¾ hours after day in. Generally well behaved, a little unsettled at first, calling out and doing small leaps. At end of patrol, Merlin became heavy in my hands and was unwilling to stop at junctions unless asked to very firmly.'

It was time for Merlin's three-month assessment. But this is not a formal examination, more of an opportunity to see how things were going in general. The return to Imber Court was a kind of working holiday. For Merlin it was a change from the daily round, a chance to consolidate his training in quieter surroundings, and to let off steam with some jumping. If there had been any problems showing up over the three months, now was the time for Jo and Karen together to resolve matters. They decided that bouncing through the daffodils was not something that could be fixed in a training school – Merlin would grow out of it. Probably.

Metropolitan Police Orders of 6 January 1859 state: 'It is a great gratification to the Commissioner that the number of police guilty of the offence of drunkenness during the late Christmas holidays has been much lower than last year. In A, F and R Divisions only one man was reported in each, and in H Division not one man was reported in the present or last year.'

Karen's diary states: 'Out to Imber Court for 3 month assessment. Merlin travelled well in box on his own. Joined remount lesson and Merlin was leading file, which he performed very well. Going through nuisances nicely until horse behind landed on a cardboard box. The noise caused Merlin to leap forward and I came out of the side door [fell off] but landing on feet and keeping hold of horse. Calm for rest of lesson. Very pleased with his nuisance work and working with five other horses.'

The next day: 'Some loose schooling before starting on one hour lesson in big school working towards some lateral movement. Once we had finished arguing with each other, established some lovely trot work on either rein. Then progressed to some leg yield and turn on forehand. Escorted Jo Sullivan's new remount Nemo on roads around Thames Ditton. Merlin behaved impeccably.

'Continuing with lateral work today. Progressed to rein back [getting the horse to move backwards, ideally in a straight line, by light touches of leg and hand]. Merlin surprised me yet again by doing it very well.'

'ON REINING BACK

'The great use of reining back has never been properly understood, and consequently not properly practised. It should not be brought into play until the horse is well bent in the neck and ribs, and obeys the pressure of the leg; during the reining back, the horse must be well in hand, and well balanced; he can then make an equal use of all four legs, and raise them equally from the ground. Before reining back see that your horse haunches to the right or left, as may be required; then give him his head and make much of him.

'It will be sufficient to practise a horse at reining back for eight days to make him do it with the greatest ease.

'At first a few steps backward is all that should be required of the horse, increasing by degrees; if he brings his hind-legs too much under him, ease the hand, and apply both legs to make him regain his balance forward; and, for this reason, always use the leg first, and then feel the reins, because, if you feel the reins first, the horse throws his weight back; and it stands to reason that the more weight he throws on his hind-legs, the less able he is to lift them, which is a necessary preliminary to stepping back; therefore, be particularly attentive in preserving the horse's balance, and, if he sticks his nose out, and hugs his tail, with his weight thrown entirely on the haunches, never attempt to rein him back, until, by applying both legs or spurs, you make him stand up again, and recover his balance – then proceed as before directed.

'The horse must never be allowed to hurry or run back out of hand, nor to diverge from a straight line.

'The squad must be frequently brought "to the right", or "to the left", when on the sides of the school, and halted near the middle, to practise the Reining Back. Do this during the Walking, Trotting and Bending Lessons; each man being told to act independent of his dressing, until all the horses rein back well.'

Captain Louis Nolan, 1852

'Trot work today was more relaxed and quicker on both reins. Finished lesson with loose school. After an hour's break, Merlin provided escort on roads for Nemo. Again he was very chilled and didn't react to anything.'

'Jumping lesson today. I found it easier to go from walk to canter and then over the jump as it stopped Merlin from getting too fizzy in the trot before we got there. Otherwise, a very honest jumper.'

And on the last day, just a little light exercise: 'A twenty minute slot in the small school this morning. Walk, trot, canter, and then I loose schooled him. Not very enthusiastic today.'

Well, maybe he was missing the bright lights. Holidays are all very well, but Merlin is not the type for doing nothing. His human equivalent would be going up the mountains for lunch, inspecting the Roman ruins before dinner, and going on to a nightclub rather than lying beside the pool all day.

Back on duty, there was the usual mixture of patrols and ceremonials, with Merlin progressing as he became more and more used to the strange behaviour of men, in particular those very odd fellows who march along banging drums and blowing trumpets, and others who jingle along on horses while dressed in shiny outfits with feathers on their heads. Escorting these colourful spectaculars through large and noisy crowds is a big part of life at Great Scotland Yard, and Merlin had to come to terms with it.

'Rear of Buckingham Palace Guard today and rear of Wellington band. Very relaxed. We joined the rear of the Queen's Life Guards from the Palace and escorted them back to the barracks. A very pleasing performance, no leaping, no excitement, very chilled.'

'Did the rear of QLG today. Met the cavalry at Hyde Park Corner and followed them to Horse Guards. Stayed on parade square. Followed rear of QLG back to Hyde Park Corner. Merlin was very calm throughout although he did find it hard to keep up with the pace of the QLG.'

'Rear of the Guard unaccompanied. He was excellent throughout. Very good with the crowds running alongside him on the pavement.'

The assumption here is that the military horses, with their very strict and narrow training, will always behave impeccably. Not so:

'3 hour patrol central Westminster walk and trot. The lead horse of the QLG started calling when he saw Merlin and Benjamin, which excited Merlin causing him to leap. He settled straight after and was excellent.'

Such things were little blips on an otherwise steady and pleasing progress. Merlin was really doing very well:

'Late turn patrol escorted by Stable Hand (Groom) Brown on Benjamin. Rode to outdoor manège at Hyde Park to do some troop drill work – half section and section walk and trot with two Hyde Park [police] horses. Merlin was well behaved and happy to work close to the other horses.'

'Stood for 30 minutes directing traffic at Kensington Gore.'

'2 hour patrol to Regents Park escorted by PC McMaster on Kathleen. Very well behaved and ignored Kathleen's strops.'

An assistant chief constable became the first chief officer for 90 years to lead a procession at the oldest festival in England. Lancashire Constabulary's ACC Peter White led the Mounted Branch procession at the 2012 Preston Guild, which was also the centenary of the Lancashire Mounted Branch.

ACC White was a member of the Mounted section when he first took part in the procession, which was at the city's last guild in 1992 – and wore the same ceremonial tunic this time. The Preston Guild is held every 20 years and dates back to the 12th century.

When ACC White met some colleagues from his mounted days, it was suggested that if he were to ride, he would be the first chief officer to lead the procession since Chief Constable Sir Harry Lane in 1922, and surely one of only a few who would have had the privilege of riding in two Guilds, 20 years apart.

ACC White said: 'I am glad to report that the ceremonial tunic I wore in 1992 still fits and, after a few training sessions, I have also got back into the swing of riding after many years away. Mastering the sword has been something a bit new, but it's all come together nicely and being part of this procession will be a great honour and something I will always be proud of as both a police officer and a Prestonian.'

When the Mounted Branch was founded, most of the officers were recruited from the cavalry of the British Army. The modern branch has 16 officers including two sergeants and 18 horses.

A veteran officer serving with Merseyside Police spoke of his pride after being chosen to lead in the winner of the Grand National at Aintree. PC Norman Edge, at the time the oldest mounted officer in the country, was joined by colleague PC Simon Griffiths at the steeplechase. PC Edge, 60, had served for 38 years while 52-year-old PC Griffiths would retire after completing 30 years' service.

Having joined Merseyside Police in 1974, PC Edge was signed up to the Mounted section in 1977 and later became responsible for training new horses joining the Force. Before starting his career with the police, the veteran officer was a Lance Corporal in the Household Cavalry, where he took part in the Trooping of the Colour and was a mounted escort at Princess Anne's wedding.

'Leading the Grand National winner in is a privilege and I am very proud,' said PC Edge. 'We are there to make sure that the winner gets into the parade ring safely. It is also a privilege just to be a mounted officer. Every time we ride in Liverpool we get people wanting to touch the horses and speak to us – there is an amazing bond.'

Every few months, the Chief Inspector of the Met Mounted Branch organises a very small parade, called the Black Escort Selection. The Met must always keep on hand a contingent of black – or very dark – horses for Royal or State funerals. They should be in matching pairs, and able to walk very slowly. Merlin went on the parade as a matter of routine but failed the test. No one could doubt his walking talents but he just wasn't dark enough. So, promotion to the spotlight would have to wait. Meanwhile, there were plenty of small incidents, usually to do with other horses: 'A few leaps when he saw the King's Troop [of the Royal Horse Artillery] and the riding school in Hyde Park'; 'Became slightly unsettled when he saw other horses'; 'Tense when escort horse walked off to take front of Guard'. Also, 'Merlin got a little anxious around Palace and Queen Victoria Memorial when he was on his own so two on Corps of Drums joined us. Settled down very well during actual guard change' and 'In school, Merlin a little naughty and not very responsive to me. More interested in the other horses.'

But against all that: '3½ hour patrol escorted by Alfie, walk and trot central Westminster and Hyde Park. Excellent. Stood still to report an accident while Alfie trotted off to catch failed-to-stop vehicle.'

Merlin was five months into duty now: 'Did rear of Buckingham Palace Guard today, not as an extra. As we were going up The Mall escorting the band, a lady fell into the road in front of us. I got off Merlin to deal with her. He stood perfectly still and was not fussed by Guard leaving without him. First time wearing chains (ceremonial dress). He got the chain in his mouth a few times so I shortened it and he was fine.'

And other notes: 'Late turn patrol escorted by PC Lindsay-Stewart on Gawain. Coming along The Mall there were a lot of roadside nuisances that upset Gawain but Merlin remained calm.' And just in case Karen Howell was getting over-confident: 'Late turn solo patrol after day in [rest day]. Merlin was excellent in traffic but we had a little argument in Lincoln's Inn Fields. He wanted to trot when I wanted him to walk, and he wanted to walk when I wanted him to trot.'

Then, after almost six months on duty: 'Solo patrol. Merlin was excellent for the first 40 minutes then for no apparent reason, on Orange Street he took off with me at a fast trot for a distance of about 15 metres until I managed to stop him by turning into a side street. I stood him still for five minutes and then we walked off. He was very heavy in my hands but he walked at my pace. He remained settled for the rest of the ride until we turned into Great Scotland Yard when he started to pull on. I stopped, made him wait and did several turns up and down the street. He eventually walked in calmly.'

Next day, whatever was bothering Merlin seemed still to be a problem: 'I attempted to do the Queen's Life Guards from the barracks but didn't get very far. Merlin was very agitated and got to the point where he was trying to barge through the cavalry horses, so I called it a day. Rode into Kensington Palace Gardens and ended up in the small outdoor school in Hyde Park. When I started schooling him he went silly and rushed into every upward transition [moving up a gait, walk to trot, trot to canter]. After about 20 minutes he gave up performing and settled into some nice work with good downwards transitions.'

And finally: 'Fairly good at rear of BPG, just a little unsettled as we approached Buckingham Palace, and leapt in the air when he saw Alfie in the distance.'

TO ACCUSTOM A HORSE TO A DRUM

Place it near him on the ground; and without forcing him; induce him to smell it again and again until he is thoroughly accustomed to it. Then lift it up, and slowly place it on the side of his neck, where he can see it, and tap it gently with a stick or your finger. If he starts, pause and let him carefully examine it. Then recommence, gradually moving it backward until it rests upon his withers, by degrees playing louder and louder, pausing always when he seems alarmed, to let him look at it and smell it if needful. In a very few minutes you may play with all your force, without his taking any notice. When this practice has been repeated a few times, your horse, however spirited, will rest his nose unmoved on the big drum while the most thundering piece is played.

In the same careful, progressive manner a horse may be accustomed to any noise or sight.

John Solomon Rarey

'Solo patrol in late afternoon. Merlin excellent on way out to Green Park. Let him eat grass. On return journey down The

Mall, Merlin started to walk faster. I turned him away and trotted up The Mall, away from home, as he was becoming stronger on our way in. After about 20 minutes of stroppiness, he settled down again and walked in quietly around Trafalgar Square.'

Everyone has good weeks and bad weeks, even police horses, and to make up for it: 'Raining on guard change today. Assisted on cordon for suspect package. Merlin good in all aspects. Merlin was ridden home by PC Thorn. Excellent behaviour, Merlin, providing an escort for me riding Katrina.'

And when another officer rode him: 'He was wonderful, a dream. Haven't had such a good ride since I was last on Merlin. You've got a real good 'un, Karen. Keep up the good work, it's all in the legs.'

This is London, a great cosmopolitan city. After 200 elephants, the next step up has to be mythical beasts: '2½ hour patrol, Lincoln's Inn Fields, Covent Garden, Soho, Chinatown. Really good. Very well behaved even when dragon was messing around.'

On ceremonial duties, it was becoming clear to everyone that there was only one place for Merlin to be – in the lead: 'Corps of Drums today. Merlin was very good on way down to barracks and, initially, when left at the gates as Kennedy went on to stop traffic. As we approached the palace, the Queen's Life Guards were heading around the Queen Victoria Memorial and this was too much for Merlin who felt he needed to be with the other horses. Merlin reared and took a massive leap. After that I could not settle him and he continued to leap about. I made the decision to move past the Guards and join Kennedy at the front. Merlin was not worried by the Guards but was more intent on being near another horse. Once at the front, ahead of Kennedy, he settled down.'

Six months later, a year from his first duty, Merlin was still making his point: 'Rode back from Queens Park Rangers football. Merlin at the back with Johnston in a column. We rode into Hyde Park at 9.30pm, in darkness, and Merlin became excited on the road into the park. He reared three times. Another horse copied Merlin and reared. The rider fell off and the horse ran away, making Merlin very excited. I dismounted and this settled him. Once the runaway was caught, I placed Merlin at the front of the column and he behaved much better. When ridden in column in the future, I suggest Merlin is kept to the front to help keep him calm.'

Chapter Five

Merlin at
the Front

During a crowd-control operation [in Chicago], a
man talking on his mobile phone refused to follow
Mounted-Police instructions to move along. Not liking
having his important call interrupted, he punched the
horse and was charged with attempting to injure same.

In the years before there was an organised police force,
the Army was used to quell the most serious cases of
public disorder. At the anti-Catholic demonstrations of
1780 (so-called 'Gordon Riots', after the leading
Protestant Lord George Gordon), troops initially
dispersed about 50,000 protesters outside Parliament
without violence. Later, the demonstrations grew into
uncontrollable rioting and the soldiers opened fire,
killing around 280 people and wounding 200 more. In
view of this, Lord Shelburne suggested that a police force

be formed along the lines of the Parisian model set up by Louis XIV in 1666, a corrupt but generally efficient system featuring mounted officers.

There were 80 more riots, some small, some large, in the following 49 years to 1829, when the first Metropolitan Police Act was passed, establishing the Metropolitan Police Force.

In any year, the Metropolitan Police has around 4,500 events of one kind or another requiring a police presence to help ensure the safety of those taking part. Many of the smaller, local ones can be handled by foot police but approaching 400 of these are big enough to warrant the deployment of the Mounted Branch, which adds up to more than 4,500 individual operations by the horses.

Some of these events are the organised annual regulars like the Mayday Parade, the Wimbledon Championships, the FA Cup Final and Community Shield, the London Marathon, and the million people at the Notting Hill Carnival. Some are predictable without being 'official', such as the celebrations in London's West End on New Year's Eve; others are the traditional tourist spectaculars like Trooping the Colour and the Changing of the Guard.

Any big march, such as the ones by Gay Pride or the Trades Union Congress, can pass off safely and peacefully but the potential for disorder is always there, as is the possibility of hijacking by groups of people with different agendas. Any large crowd also presents a marvellous opportunity for thieves, who can pick pockets and rob handbags so much more easily. On top of all that, the Met will usually have to cope with a mega-event or two. In Merlin's second year on duty, his first as a qualified and experienced public-order police horse, they had the royal wedding of Prince William and Kate Middleton and the state visit of President Barack Obama.

This type of work – public-order policing, crowd control – is one aspect of duty that above all requires slow and careful introduction. But it didn't quite work out that way for Merlin. Eight months in, and he hadn't yet attended the football or witnessed a demo, and he hadn't been on the advanced course at the Specialist Training Centre, Gravesend, where normally horses go for a day roughly every six months. The horse has to learn to put up with tennis balls and wooden bricks being thrown at him and, to make sure he gets the message, petrol bombs.

In recent decades, the Toronto Unit spent more time practising their musical ride show drills and carting around dignitaries in the landau carriage than policing. The ceremonial work was cut out in the nineties and the unit downsized (the 28 to 30 horses it maintains today are half of what it had in 1979). Staff Sergeant Patterson says it's a lean operation that provides invaluable daily policing for the investment, but the real rationale for the Unit is clear when you have 100,000 protesters heading for the Gardiner (Expressway). Even if the crowd is not hostile, there's no telling what might happen.

This was all planned for Merlin in standard sequence, but he hadn't got there yet: he was still an apprentice. Then, as the British Government announced new plans for higher education, with increased tuition fees and other measures, a big student protest brewed up.

Karen Howell: 'For one reason or another, we were short of horses. My section inspector asked me if I thought Merlin would be OK at the demo. I crossed my fingers and said yes, not at first realising it was only the horse they were interested in, not him and me as a pair. It was training out of synch. He was still officially classified as a remount, so not qualified for this job. Instead of going to school to learn it, he had to learn it in real time, and with another officer on his back.

'Of course, he'd had plenty of duty rides with many different officers but this, I thought, was a bit different. He should have had three or four footballs and at least one Gravesend session [the Metropolitan Police Specialist Training Centre], and he'd had none of that.'

Karen had every right to feel a little nervous for it would turn out to be one of the biggest demonstrations seen in London for quite some time, and one of the most emotional, as students came from all over the country to oppose the Government's spending cuts and changes in university finance. The route for the march had been approved by the police but the anticipated crowd of 20,000 soon turned into something far bigger and, in parts, uglier. Estimates of numbers of protesters on the first, very cold day, 10 November 2010, varied between 30,000 and 50,000. The initial draft of 225 police officers began to look inadequate.

The marchers moved in orderly fashion along Whitehall, past Downing Street and the Houses of Parliament, chanting and waving placards, to the rallying point outside Tate Britain (previously the Tate Gallery) on Millbank, where various speakers addressed them. On the way to the Tate, a large group, possibly several thousand, broke away. Ignoring the entreaties of their march leaders, they headed for the Tory party campaign HQ, also on Millbank. Police on foot were unable to stop an invasion, when around 200 people occupied the building, lighting fires and smashing windows while the rest of the breakaway mob cheered them on. Two officers were injured and teams in riot gear were called in to evict the occupiers, who retaliated by throwing whatever came to hand, including a fire extinguisher dropped from the roof.

According to the very experienced male PC who rode him, Merlin was 'very good, considering'. Duties included dispersing a crowd in Parliament Square, and he did get quite excited. He thought this was such fun, 'I'm enjoying it so much, I simply must eat something.' There were students at the front of the crowd wearing official vests, like breastplates, with badges on them, so Merlin grabbed a few. Otherwise, he was fine.

There was much condemnation of the violence and damage from practically everybody, including the march organisers, and with more demos planned, preparations were further-reaching. Students and others remustered, 24 November, this time including large numbers of schoolchildren. Altogether, though, numbers were fewer than before, but the police presence was far greater, and a special eye was kept out for any fringe groups bent on trouble. Lines of officers in riot gear kept the protesters away from Parliament Square. The behaviour of the majority of marchers was good humoured but there were attempts to break the police lines which had to be resisted.

Karen Howell had been reunited with Merlin, his good performance as a complete beginner in the first demo having earned him his new status as *accomplished and trustworthy under high pressure*. At around six o'clock in the evening, Mounted Police had to manoeuvre the crowds back.

Karen: 'Yes, so he'd got his boy scout's riot-proficiency badge, and on the second day we had to stand in front of a huge crowd of angry people while they jeered and shouted and threw things at us. It takes a lot of endurance, it really does. Late in the day, we were ordered to usher them away from the Houses of Parliament, a line of ten of us.'

So, there was a lot of standing still and watching, while some of the protesters lit campfires and launched missiles. This was where the placards came in useful; the organisers had delivered thousands of ready-made wood-and-board placards, ideal for waving in horses' faces, and which could be disassembled to make fire-lighting material and wooden weapons. After putting up with that all day, Merlin then had his second experience of co-ordinated action with other horses in a serial (term for a group of police working together).

Karen: 'It was quite a big ask, really, for Merlin – a horse that had never even been to a football match.'

That particular section of the crowd had proved reluctant to move in the face of about 100 officers on foot. When those police parted to allow the horses through, the protesters, seeing the mounted contingent at some distance, turned and made off. The Met was subsequently accused of a cavalry charge by students and some news reporters; possibly those witnesses had never seen a real cavalry charge, or they would not have described ten trotting police horses as such.

Karen: 'In our training, we are taught to advance at a pace that indicates we are not going to stop. So that's a fast trot or even a canter. It's a rehearsed move, called a "dispersal", and it's always supported by foot police, who move in behind us to take up the ground we've cleared.

'We have to expect missiles, expertly aimed or otherwise,

and so we have special gear for the horses to wear and, of course, they have to be trained to get used to having a guard over the nose and a visor over the eyes, plus knee and cannon-bone protectors on their legs, and a special high-visibility blanket called a quarter sheet.

'We humans have to wear body armour, with flame-resistant overalls on top, big helmets, high visibility belts, and we carry truncheons. If we feel sufficiently threatened, we can draw the truncheon and hold it aloft, called a "high-profile draw", which is meant to show that we'll use it if we have to.'

The job of the police in this situation is to facilitate peaceful demonstration, to allow the demo to happen without disrupting everybody else. Sometimes this causes violence when the cause of the demo is unpopular, such as in 1936 when the British Union of Fascists were on the march, and sometimes the numbers at the demo are so great that violent disorder is almost inevitable. And at other times the emotional nature of the cause and a sense of injustice aggravates the demonstrators into heat-of-the-moment actions they may later regret.

One factor consistent throughout all these different scenarios is that it is the police who have to deal with the problems. It's the police against whom the violence of frustration often turns, and the Mounted Police usually find themselves right up there at the front line as tempers flare.

There were more protests the following week, 30 November, in miserable wintry weather. But the march never really got underway, with the police blocking Whitehall. The demonstrators split, trying different ways to reach Parliament Square but always failing and often showing their vexation in vandalism. Many ended up in Trafalgar Square and, after a while, drifted away or were invited to leave the scene. The few who refused to go were arrested.

The last demo of the series was 9 December, when 3,000 marching students turned into 20,000 by the time they reached Parliament Square, with numbers allegedly swelled by a motley collection of activists and street gangs.

Karen: 'Among the things they threw were fireworks and paint bombs. They fill up balloons with paint, hoping to unsight the horse and the rider, and they are very messy, but even if they hit our faces it's no big deal, not the first time anyway, because my visor and Merlin's visor have plastic covers which I can tear off.'

West Yorkshire police horse Bud, a Shire-cross on duty at the football – a Newcastle-Sunderland derby match – was attacked by a Newcastle United fan. As a team of mounted officers kept large groups of fans apart after the Magpies lost the game, a man pulled his scarf up across his face and ran at Bud, trying to punch the horse on the nose. The man was arrested and restrained by police on foot, before he could land his punch. He gave his reasons for pulling the scarf over his face as feeling cold and having had a filling fall out of a tooth!

Bud received many messages of sympathy and support and suffered no damage of any kind.

From *The Guardian*: Back at Wembley (England v. Sweden, after the match), the crowd is in full flow, and a Transport for London employee warns the commanding officer that the tube station is at full capacity. He orders the other officers to turn their horses side-on to the crowd. There are still gaps in between, but when the officers raise their hands, the fans stop without protest.

It is incredibly moving to watch a line of just six horses effortlessly holding back 35,000 fans. The relationship between the police and the British public may be troubled, but judging by this night at least, it seems the force's equine members still draw a healthy respect.

On a smaller scale than riots, but with similar kinds of touch-paper waiting to be lit, are the big football matches, several of which happen in London every week of the season, and the season is a lot longer than it used to be. The police feel that the horses have a pacifying effect on crowds; what they don't want is a crowd having a non-pacifying effect on a horse. The rider is the best judge of when a young horse is ready for his first football match, and in this at least there was no horse shortage to mess up the schedules.

Karen: 'We continued with his training the correct way, and it was Fulham. Normal duty at the football can last for nine hours. Not nine hours on the horse's back, but that length of time together, including all the stable work at both ends of the duty. At some night games, pouring with rain and freezing cold, by the time you've done the odd jobs at the end, cleaning all your tack and haying round, it's one o'clock in the morning.

'But you don't start off like that. We rode there, which is a two-hour trip, planning to keep pretty much in the background and only to stay until half-time. Two hours is a good amount of exercise anyway, and then we stood around as the fans went in, no problems there, and I gave him a bag of feed, a bucket of water from a tap in the nearest police station yard, and we rode home.'

The job at the football is to prevent trouble, and key to that is keeping the rival fans apart. After a few more outings to absorb the atmosphere, Merlin was ready.

Karen: 'It depends where we are, obviously, but the first thing is usually to patrol the area around the ground, where we might find opportunists looking to break into the parked cars – it's classic crime prevention, and with an excellent vantage point. As it gets nearer to kick-off time, we might be escorting large groups of fans coming out of the nearest tube station. These will be the away supporters, and we're there to stop the home fans getting too close, so you're protecting them from each other, and you try to get everyone safely to the ground without any fights starting. Fights are like fires: they're relatively easy to put out if you catch them soon enough, but once they get a hold they can explode into something uncontrollable.

'Once everybody's in and the match starts, that's the horses' break time. We feed and water and just hang around, hoping there are no inflammatory incidents on the field. If there is any crowd trouble, it is generally after the game, caused by something that happened in the match. A footballer gets a red card – quite right too, thinks one lot of fans – a total case of cheating, injustice and provocation, thinks the other lot. Or, there was a disallowed goal, or the home side losing, or the away side losing, or maybe someone has had a few sherbets too many, or a combination of all of that.'

'I was on duty at Deepdale [Preston, Lancashire] when North End were playing Sheffield United, and the thousands of visiting fans were pouring out after the match. Mounted Branch were there, doing an excellent job as usual – just showing the heavy hoof is usually enough on its own. Anyway, in among this vast sea of red and white there was somebody one of the mounted officers didn't like the look of, so he shouted, "Hey, you there, you in the red scarf!" It was quite amusing, watching 500 people all look up at once.'

Police Constable, Lancashire

Karen: 'Merlin and I have had to sort out a few little local difficulties. When I spot something happening, some kind of fight kicking off, I want to be in there before it turns into a pitched battle, and so I push Merlin to a trot and we go for it. The crowd parts in front of us, and suddenly the warring factions forget what they were fighting about while I try to stop Merlin pinching a scarf or a woolly hat. The fans don't attack us, or very rarely; they are very wary of the horses. I've never had to use my truncheon.

'Not all crowds behave according to the manual. The pro-hunt demonstrators, for example, offered a new slant on things. A lot of them had never been on a demo before, so they weren't quite as street-wise as the ones you sometimes get, but they also had no fear of horses. They knew all about horses, and especially big hunter types like Merlin. They were not intimidated but neither were they likely to throw stuff and try to hurt him. Mind you, one did try to pull a horse's headgear off, but the officer soon put a stop to that.

'Another different sort of crowd is the rugby lot at Twickenham. Some of them are country people as well, maybe, but really it's the attitude that's different. You know,

"We're rugby chaps, not your soccer hooligans. We don't need police. So what are you doing here? Clear off and do something useful!"'

The police Mounted Unit in Chicago has 32 horses, and 27 of them were released from their stables one late evening in September 2012. A 20-year-old horse, named JR after the *Dallas* anti-hero, was sprayed in the eyes with a fire extinguisher and another, called Schott, was cut on the leg by a fire extinguisher thrown at him.

'The intruders did not come to commit a theft; rather, they came to maliciously harm our horses, for what reason, I don't know,' explained Lieutenant Paul Bauer, commander of the unit. The incident happened on a Sunday night. After veterinary treatment, the two injured horses were back on duty on the Tuesday.

TO INSPECTOR TURNER, 1 UNIT GSY, GREAT SCOTLAND YARD

Merlin (184) has been out to duty since March 2010 and is competent in all aspects of his work. He has attended football matches on several occasions including Arsenal and Chelsea as well as rugby at Twickenham. He was also involved in several of the student demonstrations in December 2010. On each occasion he has performed well, working on his own and with other horses.

Merlin is able to do the front of the QLG and is working towards doing the front of the Wellington and St James's bands. He has completed several trotting escorts and is at ease with all other aspects of the ceremonial duties performed on 1 Unit.

Merlin has attended POTC and performs to a satisfactory level.

I therefore request that Merlin may now be shown as an Operational Police Horse from the date of this report.

Submitted for your consideration.

PC 382 Karen Howell

Chapter Six

Merlin in the Limelight

To promote tourism, the Kaohsiung County Government (Taiwan) has organised a Mounted Police team. The Changhua County Government in central Taiwan is planning to take the same action for its Lukang Township, an ancient port city and a major gate for earlier Chinese immigrants to settle in Taiwan, centuries ago.

BALTIMORE, MARYLAND, USA, DECEMBER 1943

Whether leading a parade, or in service breaking traffic jams, the mounted division is among the most colourful divisions of the Baltimore Police Department and always attracts the attention of the pedestrians. During the almost 40 years of its existence, the mounted division has been gradually bettered until today with its 17 men and officers, not to mention the horses, it is probably the best mounted division in the country. It is a part of the traffic division and therefore is under direct command of Captain Henry Kaste. For years uncounted, its principal activities have been confined to Light and Pratt Streets, where shipping matters engage the labours of the various trucking concerns. Years ago it was thought that the widening of Light Street would care for any traffic problems but increased business on the street has made the work of the mounted officers more responsible. Further north, Baltimore, Eutaw, Howard and Lexington Streets require the attention of the Mounted division. But at the head of a parade men and horses come into their own and reflect great credit on the police department.

The Queen's Life Guards ride every day from Knightsbridge Barracks to Horse Guards Parade, and back again. At Buckingham Palace the Changing of the Guard also happens every day in the summer, every other day in winter, and the Mounted Branch based at Great Scotland Yard provides escorts for all these occasions. It's an important thing to learn for all new horses there, embracing crowd control, security and criminal activity by pickpockets and others who prey on the crowd. So, how would Merlin cope with this?

Karen Howell: 'I knew this was going to take some time, because of his constant wish to be with other horses, and here was a whole tribe of them in military formation, all behaving perfectly most of the time, and I was on a horse that could ruin the entire spectacle.

'My plan was to let him look at the Guards from a distance,

and gradually get closer. He got so excited, jumping up and down, just being silly, that I could see it was going to take even longer than I'd thought. But, we kept going, until he was used to it and realised that it wasn't his show.'

From the diary, two months into Merlin's probation: 'Saw Royal Mews carriage go past and managed to behave himself. Went and stood with horses of Queen's Life Guards and left them calmly. Waited outside the Palace when QLG went past. No reaction to seeing other horses or them passing him.'

Excellent reports for the next three days led to a rest day for Merlin, which often meant a little over-enthusiasm when he went back to work.

Diary: 'Did an hour walk and trot patrol before attempting to do rear of QLG. Merlin stood nicely with the QLG horses and was happy to stand while QLG came out from Horse Guards Parade. Unfortunately the sound of the bollards coming down upset him and he did a huge leap. I moved off with the QLG but Merlin was clearly unsettled and continued to leap forwards.'

Karen had to take him away and, after riding through Birdcage Walk and Grosvenor Gardens, did 45 minutes of routines in the Household Cavalry outdoor school: 'Merlin performed very well in school and was responsive and attentive. One more leap on way home due to sound of metal gate closing behind him.'

Two days later, Karen tried again: '2 hour patrol escorted by PC Pitt on Intrepid. Followed rear of QLG at a distance. Merlin very calm. Stood in The Mall while the picket came by. Again Merlin remained alert but calm. Walked past the band playing, no problems. Trotted in half section [as a pair] with two other horses in front. Merlin was impeccably behaved.'

'1¾ hour patrol escorted by PC Baker on Headley. Did first part of Corps of Drums [guard-changing band. 'First part' is leading the soldiers carrying but not playing their instruments, from Wellington Barracks to St James's Palace, ready for the start of the Change proper]. Merlin was tense at first but then relaxed down and followed the band happily along The Mall. Returned home alone via Parliament Square and Whitehall. After initial whinny on leaving Headley, Merlin settled and walked in very relaxed.'

'3½ hour walk/trot patrol with PC Baker on Katrina. Followed Corps of Drums first part. Went into St James's Palace to mingle with band. Watched Corps of Drums leave Wellington Barracks and followed along Spur Road. Watched new Guard leave and followed along The Mall. All very good apart from two leaps and one attempted leap while trotting home. Turned him around and continued trotting. Very good.'

From a Taiwan newspaper: 'Police officers on horseback patrolled the streets of Taipei County capital Banqiao City for the first time yesterday after the crack mounted police team made its debut five years ago. From now on, the mounted police will expand their patrol territory on the weekends and public holidays.

'In addition to maintaining public order, the mounted police will become part of the public scenery. To the delight and surprise of both children and adults, the mounted police officers in crisp uniform and their tall horses became the most popular company of people who like to take pictures.

'Many children were thrilled by the unexpected

appearance of real horses on the "malu" – the common Chinese term for road, which actually translates as 'horse road' (ma – horse, lu – road) – right in front of their eyes. The bolder kids reached out to touch the huge animals for a rare experience.

'The daily patrol hours on the malu are from 9 to 11am in the morning and 3 to 5pm, in the areas of Zhongshan Road, Minquan Road, Wenhua Road, and Xinjan Road. Mounted police members and their horses will also make a 30-minute stop from 9.20am to 9.50am at County Citizen Plaza in the morning for people who like to take photos or pose with the horses. They will make a similar stop at the Banqiao Station Plaza from 3.20pm to 3.50pm.'

South Yorkshire Police's latest equine recruit went to meet the youngsters responsible for giving him his official South Yorkshire Police name, Treeton.
Treeton the police horse and his trainer and rider, PC Alison Akers, visited Class Four of Treeton Primary School, chosen out of more than 60 entries submitted when South Yorkshire Police invited residents of South Yorkshire to name its new police horse.

Treeton is seven years old and is a black and white Shire cross warmblood. He has been through a number of public order training sessions, has helped police the county's town centres and already worked his first football matches.

PC Alison Akers said: 'Treeton was brought in to replace police horse Hallam, who retired earlier this year after 17 years' service, so he had big shoes to fill. So far, he is settling in well and is showing that he has the ideal temperament to be a police horse, including taking a classful of excited schoolchildren in his stride.'

Karen Howell: 'Merlin's job was to follow the Guards, and quietly, so I could deal with the traffic, and then his job was to lead them, and eventually he cottoned on. All those other horses, they follow me, and this is my job. Now, after three years at it, he sees himself absolutely as the leader – I'm in front, the rest of you fall in behind. And if Karen puts me at the back, I'll make life difficult until she realises what is my rightful place.'

Perhaps it's not a thought that occurs to many when watching a royal wedding or another big occasion on the television, but the carriage horses and drivers did not reach such a standard of faultless behaviour with just a couple of practice runs. They train long and hard and, like the police, have to prove themselves on the streets. This not only applies to the great ceremonials; the royal carriages are used to convey ambassadors and high commissioners from their official residences to the Palace, to present their credentials to HM the Queen, and there are about 50 such outings in a year.

Twice a year, the new carriagemen have their Final Drive, which is from the Royal Mews behind the Palace to the old King's Troop barracks in St John's Wood and back again. It's a 40–45 minute trot both ways, with the drivers being assessed on how they do with a four-in-hand. The Met Mounted Branch form the escort, finding a way through the traffic with no special arrangements beforehand, looking to solve any problems that might otherwise upset the chances of success for those taking this very unusual driving test.

The standard method is for two police riders to lead and one to follow. One of the two in front will go on ahead, stop the traffic and deal with any obstacles and interruptions while the other sees the parade through the next set of lights. Standard methods were not, it would seem, Merlin's methods.

Karen Howell: 'When it was Merlin's first time at this, knowing him, I said we had to be at the front – Merlin would be a nuisance if he had to follow behind this new arrangement of horses. So we set off from the Royal Mews, at a trot, and he thought, "This is really good fun" and broke into a canter. I tried to stop him, so he turned sideways. He was cantering sideways, looking at the carriage horses behind him.

'This really would not do. If we'd been behind he'd have wanted to catch up. In front, he wanted to go back and join the others. I had to admit defeat. I called to the other officer that I was giving up, that she would have to manage, and I turned Merlin and walked him away into the back streets. I set off for home and then thought, "Hang on, Merlin. You are not getting away with this. You have been very naughty, you've shown me up, and I'm not standing for it. You are not going to muck me about. You can do this job, I know you can, and you are jolly well going to do it."

'So, we took a short cut, through Green Park. I knew the route so I knew where we could join up again, and we did. The other officer said she saw me coming at speed through the gates with a look of determination on my face. Merlin was a bit out of breath, but never mind. We settled in to our position and carried on as if nothing had happened.'

The Changing of the Guard at Buckingham Palace is one of the major tourist attractions in London, and it's an everyday duty in the summer for the horses based at Great Scotland Yard, and every other day in winter. They are all supposed to learn how to do it, and some become better than others.

It starts with a military band and a troop of Guards on foot leaving Friary Court, by St James's Palace, escorted down The Mall to Buckingham Palace by two mounted officers at the front and two behind. This group, which is the detachment of the Old Guard on duty at St James's, must join the Buckingham detachment at the Palace at 11.25am, entering by the south centre gate (on the left as you look from The Mall) and so completing the Old Guard for inspection.

The New Guard, also with a band, now marches the short distance from Wellington Barracks, Birdcage Walk, to arrive at 11.30am, escorted by one mounted officer front and rear. While the actual changing happens, with the symbolic handing over of the Palace keys and the posting of sentries, the band plays a programme of popular music. This takes something over half an hour, while the mounted officers keep the crowds clear of the gates and watch out for the pickpockets and bag snatchers who attend these ceremonials so religiously. Horseback arrests are quite common.

With the change complete, the Old Guard leaves by the centre gate with its Mounted Police escort and heads for Wellington Barracks, and the St James's detachment of the New Guard heads for the other palace, similarly escorted.

There's another Changing of the Guard before this, when the Queen's Life Guards (Household Cavalry) make their daily progress from Knightsbridge (Hyde Park) Barracks, leaving at 10.28am (09.28am on Sundays) to arrive at Horse Guards Parade at a minute or two before 11am (10am on

Sundays). Horse Guards is the official entry point to the royal residences at Buckingham Palace and St James's Palace, as established by Charles II. The somewhat longer journey is escorted by three mounted officers riding in the centre of the road. One goes well ahead, checking unattended vehicles and stopping traffic. The second rides immediately in front of the Guards, and the third follows up behind, marshalling traffic past the marchers.

The route could hardly be more challenging, especially as the Guards are not supposed to come to a standstill. They go along Constitution Hill and The Mall, but must negotiate Hyde Park Corner to get there, where there is traffic in five lanes and then three lanes, all of which has to be stopped by one police officer, such as Karen Howell, on one police horse, such as Merlin.

When the new guard arrives at Horse Guards, if HM the Queen is at home, their trumpeters and those of the old guard sound the Royal Salute, and again when the old guard leaves.

The Duke of Wellington was having so much trouble with unruly soldiers in the Peninsular War that he decided some form of police force was necessary to stop the looting, drunkenness and general mayhem. The result was a Staff Corps of Cavalry under a Provost Marshal but, like other policing initiatives of the time, the Force was too small to make much difference.

The Corps had no special uniform at first, and so wore a red favour tied around the right arm while riding in their normal regimental dress. Napoleon defeated, the Corps was disbanded to be reformed as the Mounted Staff Corps during the Crimean War, with the same purpose: to enforce discipline and stop thievery. Their results may have been better, as they were mostly men recruited from the Irish Constabulary, plus some from the Metropolitan Police.

Another small force was established around the same time: the Military Mounted Police, who were soldiers from Guards and Hussars regiments, and they became a permanent fixture in 1877, with 75 NCOs and men, and 71 horses. The formation of the Military Foot Police came shortly after.

The famous red cap cover came into use before the First World War. During that conflict, a much enlarged and hastily recruited MP [Military Police] force acquired a poor reputation among many ordinary soldiers. Part of police duty was to prevent desertion and to catch those who did desert, whose court martials so often resulted in a death sentence (only 10 per cent of which were carried out).

The two corps, Mounted and Foot, were integrated in 1926 as the Corps of Military Police, which became the Corps of Royal Military Police in 1946. The Mounted Branch declined in numbers before the Second World War as mechanised transport took over, although some horses remained in outposts of Empire. Disbanded in 1945, the Mounted Branch was re-established in 1950. Mounted MPs certainly had uses in rough country but theirs were mainly ceremonial duties. The unit, then only 20 strong, was finally closed down in 1995.

*

Like everything else, such escort duty has to be introduced slowly. Diary: 'Patrolled Piccadilly and Green Park, then watched old Guard from stable yard, then followed to Buckingham Palace. Stayed at Palace for Guard change, saw new Guard arrive. Policed Guard change with Flintlock as escort. Followed at rear of Wellington Guard. No problems at all.'

'Escorted by PC Bruce on Gawain. Patrolled Belgravia before Guard change. Did rear of St James Guard then rear of Wellington band. Merlin very chilled even when Wellington band came out early in front of him. Watched QLG go past. Finished off Guard change at rear of St James's Guard back to St James's Palace. A very pleasing performance.'

'Did rear of guard change and guard environs. An extremely relaxed, tired horse, not fazed by anything.'

Merlin was first-class on most days, but he retained his quirkiness. He knew when he was supposed to behave but occasionally forgot.

Karen Howell: 'He's perfectly happy in the lead. The band's behind him, everything's fine, except when we're with Lionheart; they're like naughty schoolboys together. "I don't know, today I'm a bit bored, so let's get Lionheart jumping about a bit" – you can see them looking at each other, almost as if it's a conspiracy. Let's liven things up a little.'

While the ceremonials and pageantry are important for Great Scotland Yard horses, ordinary police work is still their main occupation. After three months on duty, Merlin was beginning to show that he'd grasped the essentials and, maybe, he could even show the others a thing or two.

Diary: 'Out twice today. Rode on outside of Katrina, south of river. Excellent despite Katrina's reactions to buses. Then provided escort for Messenger. Again, Merlin behaved impeccably and ignored Messenger's leaps.'

Merlin enjoyed this work, especially the contact with spectators, and became very good at it. Would this mean he could be trusted with a prominent role at a certain wedding that was coming up?

Initially, Merlin's job at the biggest ceremonial event for years, the wedding, on 29 April 2011, of HRH Prince William and Miss Kate Middleton, was as a security measure, in the background. The route for the procession to and from Westminster Abbey, which would be lined by over a million spectators, had been the subject of an enormous amount of security planning. It would be as heavily policed on the day as was compatible with the nature of the occasion, by visible and not so visible officers, but there had to be a Plan B. Despite every possible measure being taken, something could go wrong and if it did, the procession might be forced to divert.

Karen and Merlin were to patrol Horse Guards Avenue; ready to lead the carriages down that way, should the need arise. Of course, everything went like the proverbial clockwork and so the next job was another kind of leadership, for those many thousands and thousands of people who had got themselves into position at the top of The Mall.

Once the royal party and all the company had gone down The Mall, the Mounted Branch had to form a line across the road. With the crowd in order behind, they would slowly approach the Palace gates, so that everyone could be there in time for the balcony appearance. The estimated worldwide television audience for this was over two billion. It was Merlin's greatest moment so far!

Karen: 'There were 12 of us in the line. We walked down The Mall, with what seemed like the whole world following.'

Merlin was superb. Well, it was ideal for him – after all, he was showing the way. But what would happen when they got there?

Karen: 'Merlin and I, with the chief inspector and two sergeants, then formed the quartet of Mounted Police standing at the main gate, in the centre, with the balcony right behind us.'

Merlin had only recently graduated from trainee to operational police horse. The noise and the excitement were beyond anything he'd experienced. Now he wasn't leading the crowd, he was facing them – and what a lot of people. Talk about a sea of faces, this was a potential tidal wave.

'There was nowhere to go: we couldn't go backwards into the Palace, we couldn't go forwards with the biggest, most clamorous crowd in front. I just said a silent prayer: "Please, Merlin, be a good boy."

'Just as I thought the noise couldn't get any louder, the happy couple appeared on the balcony. The crowd went absolutely mad, cheering, shouting, cameras flashing, thousands of flags waving. Then the Queen came out and all the rest of the family, and the noise went up another notch, and the waving and flashing went further up the crazy scale. Then William and Kate kissed and wow, up it went again. Well, I'd never seen or heard anything like it in all my years in the police. Absolute madness! Nice madness, but still awe-inspiring. I cannot imagine what it must have seemed like to Merlin. If he served a hundred years he'd never experience anything more intimidating. And then, at the peak of everything, we had the fly-past.'

First came the Lancaster, the Spitfire and the Hurricane of the Battle of Britain Memorial Flight (powered, as it happens, by Rolls-Royce Merlin engines), followed by four jets – two Tornado GR4S and two Typhoons. After the allotted six minutes, with a final wave from William and Kate, the balcony party disappeared and that was it.

It's all on YouTube, if readers want to see it. That's PC Karen Howell on Merlin, the rightmost of the four horses as you look towards the Palace gates. Number of views: a million squillion.

'We spent the next hour and a half trying to get the crowd away from the front of the Palace. Nothing more to see, please move on. People were reluctant to go. I guess some were hoping to see the honeymoon couple leaving in their car, but that was not on the agenda. Anyway, it was all resolved in great good humour. It had been a long day, and Merlin was utterly fantastic throughout.'

Merlin had come of age. Nothing could faze him ever again. Probably. Now he was a proper police horse as well as a TV star, and he had been noticed in upper circles.

Buckingham Palace became mere routine to Merlin but he could still pull out the occasional surprise. *Your Horse* magazine wanted to do a 'day in the life' piece on a police horse and Merlin, with Karen, was selected for the starring role. Everything went normally until the half-hour interlude between journeys, when officer and horse wait outside the Palace, keeping an eye out for thieves and vagabonds. It was a lovely sunny day and nothing much was happening, so Merlin decided to eat a traffic cone.

Finding that he couldn't actually eat it, he dropped it neatly on top of another. The *Your Horse* photographer knew he was on to a winner. Merlin became the police horse that stacks traffic cones and had his own feature in the *Daily Mail*.

Karen: 'He'd picked up cones before, though he'd never stacked them. It was pure luck, but it made everybody's day.'

Turkish media reported in 2012 that the National Police Department was to introduce Mounted Police in the cities of Ankara, zmir and Antalya to patrol events such as festivals, demonstrations and football matches.

There have long been Mounted Police in Turkey but these have been deployed mainly in rural areas. The new, city-based units are being introduced as part of the country's harmonisation process with the European Union, as part of the membership negotiations.

The police department has done extensive research into the Mounted Police of Denmark, Belgium, the Netherlands, Great Britain, Austria, Germany and France, with the intention of bringing Turkish rural and city mounted squads into accord with international standards.

Mounted Police will serve where motor vehicles cannot – for example, in parks, outside football stadiums and entertainment arenas, at festival grounds and other events drawing large crowds. The horses will undergo training, featuring percussion bombs, tear gas, noisy traffic and fire.

The Mounted Police will also support projects around disabled children, in which equestrian therapy can have positive effects.

To paraphrases an American historian, Veronyka James: Police departments in Australia created mounted patrol units in the 19th century, responsible for most law enforcement in the gold fields during the 1850 gold rush, controlling rioting in Sydney and finding runaway convicts. To the present day, mounted patrols in Australia conduct searches for missing persons and escaped prisoners in wilderness areas, and seek out drug plantations and stolen cattle.

There are some Mounted jobs that have to be done with a senior police officer on the horse's back rather than the normal partner. The senior officer in question will – obviously – be able to ride, but will not be one who does so every day. Selection of horses for such duties is an important matter, bearing in mind the many possibilities for said senior officer to be made to look a fool by a misbehaving animal.

One example of these nerve-jangling events is the State Opening of Parliament. In our case, a Deputy Assistant Commissioner of the Met had to appear on horseback, wearing a special (and especially uncomfortable) uniform, ceremonial feathers and whatnot. Naturally, no one wants to be made to look an idiot on a prancing horse but the possibilities of disaster go way beyond that. Imagine the years of mickey taking by thousands of police officers. Imagine the newspaper headlines *and* the pictures. Inquiries were made and the answer was Merlin.

As well as the DAC's historical outfit, the horse had to have unusual accoutrements including a ceremonial sword, a dress-uniform numnah [under-saddle sheepskin] and a feathery item called 'The Beard' that hangs down from the horse's head-dress and, of course, Merlin wanted to eat it.

Karen Howell: 'That took a lot of doing. I had to go out with him numerous times, wearing this beard thing, and I did get him to ignore it but he was still liable to be tempted. When I saw him going for it, I gave him a little slap with my hand on his shoulder. "Good as gold," I told the DAC. "Just remember, if he goes for the beard, just lean forward and give him a little tap on the shoulder." Out she went to the ceremony, and back she came with a big smile on her face.'

But there was more to that smile than simple pleasure that the show had gone well. The previous year, on a different horse, had been rather embarrassing. There is a point in the ceremony when the Royal Navy contingent is called to attention. The horse was used to the Guards regiments on ceremonial duties, when calls to attention, much practised for public consumption, sound to the horse like a single gunshot. The Navy are not Guardsmen, they don't do square-bashing drills to the same extent: when they stand to attention, they are not necessarily all to the exact split second and, on this occasion, the horse took a dislike to the new sound and shot across Parliament Square, taking the DAC with him. So, when Merlin took no notice of the sailor boys, the DAC was very glad of it.

When the Olympic Games came to London, it was the largest peacetime safety and security operation ever mounted in the UK, taking years of planning and lasting for 105 days, from 4 June 2012 when the security searches began, to 16 September 2012 when the Paralympic Village closed. On the busiest days there were 9,500 police officers on duty, and every day 50 mounted officers were deployed.

As well as standard Mounted Branch work on a much larger scale than usual, there was the Our Greatest Team Parade on 10 September, watched by millions on television around the world, as well as by masses of people in the street. By now it was clear that Merlin, while still the mischievous joker of old, seemed to know when he certainly had to behave impeccably and do the job.

Around 800 Olympic and Paralympic competitors rode on 21 lorries, parading through London over a two-hour route, from Mansion House, Ludgate Hill, Fleet Street, along The Strand, past Charing Cross, Trafalgar Square, down The Mall, lined by a crowd estimated to be in the hundreds of thousands, and finishing up at the Queen Victoria Memorial, outside Buckingham Palace, with a flypast including the Red Arrows in the sky and a pop concert and speeches on the ground.

Leading them all the way were several extremely noisy bands, two enormous lion heads, and the Chief Inspector of the Metropolitan Police Mounted Branch, on Merlin.

PC Trudi Gunn was one of many extra police drafted into London for the Olympics: 'I am a mounted officer from Avon and Somerset in London to help police the Olympics, along with the rest of my team and our horses. The horse I am riding today [Saturday, 11 August 2012] is called Clifton. He is 13 years old, 17 hands high and has been a police horse for 8 years.

'The horses we have brought up from Avon and Somerset have coped really well with the number of people in London. I'm used to patrolling Bristol, which in many ways is similar to policing London, but London is a lot bigger, a lot busier – it never seems to stop here. Today, I have been patrolling the live site at Hyde Park. We love it when people come up and say hello, and Clifton loves it when they bring him mints. The live site is very busy today, with fantastic weather. There have been lots of families with picnics and with another Gold [Mo Farah's second, in the 5,000 metres] in the stadium there has been a great atmosphere. We have all loved being here, enjoying the excitement with all of the visitors today.'

Chapter Seven

Merlin in
the Field

O ne of the benefits of Mounted Police that cannot be
counted, tabulated or put on a balance sheet is the
goodwill generated. The early riding drills of the North
West Mounted Police (forerunners of the Royal
Canadian Mounted Police, the 'Mounties') in 19th-
century Canada soon developed into public exhibitions
of horsemanship and, in the 1870s, someone thought of
setting this to music. Until 1966, horse riding was part of
the training for all new Mounties but nowadays the only
horsemanship is for the show, the Musical Ride, and
some ceremonial duties and parades.

For the Musical Ride, a troop of 32 riders and horses
perform intricate figures and cavalry drill, in twos, fours
and eights, at the trot and at the canter, requiring months
of training. One of the formations, 'The Dome', used to
feature on the back of the Canadian 50-dollar bill, but

the highlight is the charge when lances, with their red and white pennons, are lowered and the riders launch into the gallop. The conclusion is the march past as the band plays the RCMP's Regimental March.

The Musical Ride tours throughout Canada and to some international venues, performing around 50 times a year between May and October.

The RCMP breeds its own horses at 16 to 17 hands, traditionally from registered thoroughbred stallions and part-thoroughbred mares. In 1989, Black Hannoverians were brought in to improve bloodlines. Horses begin their training at three years of age and at age six, join the Musical Ride. The maple leaf pattern on the horses' rumps is created by brushing across the lie of the hair with a damp brush over a stencil.

Noel McCarthy was a sergeant in the Met Mounted Branch who was killed in a motorcycle accident on his way to work. The Met's annual day of riding displays and competitions is named in his honour, the Noel McCarthy Trophy Day.

September 2012: the sun shines brightly on the Imber Court showground. There are tents, music, a table loaded with silver trophies, and another table with notices proclaiming a sale of cakes although the cakes have not appeared yet (the Mounted Branch seems rather fond of cakes). The penalty for falling off your horse while on duty is to bring in cakes for everyone the next day.

The first event, Best Turn-out, doesn't feature Merlin as it's for officers with less than five years' service in the Mounted Branch. He won't feature in it next year either, as his new partner due to take over from Karen Howell next spring, PC

Paul Hyde (known as 'Jecks', short for Jekyll), will have more than five years in by then. PC Hyde's current mount, Benjamin, is a 20-year-old, 'brilliant at all the ceremonial stuff but he hates large crowds, so he's no good at the football. They all have their strengths and weaknesses – well, almost all, and that's Benjamin's. They say Merlin is good at everything, so next year I'll be going to the football more often.'

For the Best Turn-out, five horses stand patiently in line abreast while the appropriately named Inspector Russell Pickin looks for tiny faults in the horses' grooming and tack, and in the officers' uniforms. They all look superb, so if the Inspector is going to pick faults, they will be little ones.

Next up is a big event, Troop Drill, featuring Merlin but ridden by PC Alex Richards. This is a team event – four teams, one made up of the trainers, three representing combinations of the Met's stables. Merlin's team is drawn from Great Scotland Yard and Hyde Park stations. No one really starts off as favourite as such a lot can go wrong but, according to a whisper, the trainers should be the weakest team since they don't practise this sort of thing much.

Troop Drill manoeuvres are based on cavalry movements used on the battlefield, with a great deal of forming and reforming. In single file, sections and half sections, they wheel in a 90-degree turn, peel off to the left and right at 45 degrees, form a line abreast going forward, wheel again, all to orders shouted by the judge.

The movements are familiar but the sequence of them is a surprise today, to test them out. Wheeling is especially difficult; the horse at one end of the line is almost stationary while the rest have to go faster, the further out they are. They advance in pairs, turn to make a heart shape, all the while watching for 'dressing' – keeping up with the pace, all maintaining the same gait, and not allowing gaps, and not allowing the opposite either: the concertina effect. In crowd control, there must be no large spaces between horses for aggressive individuals to dive through. The regulation spacing is six inches from officer's knee to officer's knee when they're in section, half section or line abreast. When sections are one behind another, there should be four feet between noses and tails. These are the old, traditional measurements – 121.92 centimetres doesn't quite hack it.

That gap is bound to vary as they change from one formation to another. What counts is how quickly and neatly they close up again. Now they wheel again, and the outside rider gets left behind. They reform, with more turns, and reassemble again into twos and fours. To the untutored eye, it all looks as well co-ordinated as the synchronised swimmers at the Olympics, but here, as at the Games, there are judges who spot every foible, every little mistake, and every instance when the horse does not do exactly as instructed.

They finish with a line-abreast fast canter towards the showground railings, and stop in a perfect atten-shun! Well, nearly perfect.

The general opinion was that Merlin's team had had one or two too many concertinas, gaps, wide man on the wheel being left behind, hesitations, deviations and repetitions of deviations, and the judges agreed. The winners were the alleged least favourites, the trainers of Imber Court. Perhaps the best riders didn't need so much practice.

The *Technique de Randonnée Equestre de Competition* (method of competition in horse-trekking), thankfully known as TREC, or Le TREC, was developed in the 1970s as a means of training and testing French equestrian guides who lead groups of people on riding holidays. Adapted all across the equestrian world, it now forms the basis for testing many different types of rider, including police officers. There is an orienteering section to it that the police miss out; otherwise they follow the broad concepts of *Maîtrise des Allures* (mastership of gaits), called Control of Paces, and *Parcours en Terrain Varié* (riding over a varied course), the obstacle section. The Met have incorporated this into a Best Trained Horse competition as part of the Noel McCarthy Day, and Merlin was entered for it, ridden by PC Karen Howell. So how did he get on?

Spurs and whips are not allowed during the TREC event; it's all in the hands and legs. Sixteen horses were entered, some ridden by the Imber Court trainers.

Phase One – Control of Paces. Horses had to canter and walk over a short course, 60 metres, and could circle before starting to establish the gait. Part 1 – Slowest Canter: Merlin had to canter between two stakes placed in the ground (at which point the judge started the watch), then follow the show-ring fence around the corner at the slowest possible canter but without breaking gait into a trot, over a distance of 60 metres, and through the second set of stakes, when the watch was stopped. Points out of 30 would be awarded, and the slowest time of the day would win.

Merlin would not win the slowest canter. His time was slow enough but he dropped out of canter at one stage. As they used to say on the Eurovision Song Contest: Merlin, nul points.

THE HORSE'S PACES – WALK, TROT AND CANTER

The Walk: If a horse walks well, his action is generally good and by bringing the principles of this system into play, first at a walk, you regulate and improve his other paces.

Before moving forward, the horse should be light in hand, the head brought home, the neck arched, and he should stand evenly on both hind-legs. Close the legs and communicate a sufficient impulse to carry him forward, but do not ease the hand at the same time, as laid down in the old system, because if you do, the head and neck may relapse into a position which will defy the control of the hand.

The bit should be to the horse an insurmountable obstacle whenever he attempts to get beyond the position to which he is reined in; he never tries it without suffering, and it is only within its limits that he can find himself at ease. The rider should therefore always have a light feeling of both reins, and when the horse bores on the bit, keep the hand steady; use both legs, which, by bringing his haunches under him, will oblige the horse to take his weight off your hand.

Perfect him in his **Walk** before you try to do so at a **Trot** and a **Gallop** for this simple reason: he has three points to rest on when at a walk (as he lifts but one leg at a time), and can easily maintain his balance; and while his action is so little brought into play, he is more susceptible of the different impressions we wish to convey. Therefore, combine the use of hand and leg to collect him and improve his carriage, and assist in uniting the play of the forehand and haunches.

To keep up the **Walk** at an even pace, it is necessary that the impulsive and controlling powers emanating from the rider be in perfect harmony.

Suppose you require a power equal to 20 pounds to move the horse forward, of which 15 pounds is for the impulsive power and 5 pounds to keep the horse reined in; if the legs communicate a greater impulse, without the hand augments the resistance in proportion, it is evident that what is in excess will be thrown on the forehand, and then the horse is no longer light in hand. If, on the contrary, the hand seizes on too large a share (or in other words, is too heavy), it will impede the horse in his forward course, slacken the pace and interfere with his carriage. This goes far to show how hand and leg must work together from the beginning, though of course in a different degree, according to the horse.

The Trot: A horse trots when he raises the off fore and the near hind leg, or near fore and off hind, from the ground at the same time. Those paces at which the horse is most easily balanced must precede the ones in which it is more difficult to retain him in equilibrium; therefore, after the **Walk**, begin with a steady, collected **Trot**.

It is necessary, in order to make the horse handy, to exercise him at 'Trotting out', but it is not enough that he should trot fast; the quickness of pace should not detract from his lightness in hand, nor the ease with which he should be capable of answering all indications of hand and leg. The hand must be constantly at work to retain the head and neck in their proper position, without counteracting the forward impulse communicated by the leg; and thus the horse placed between two powers (hand and leg), which only oppose his bad qualities, will soon develop his good ones, and acquire regularity of pace, increased speed and that safety which is natural to a horse well balanced and light in hand. In speaking here of increased speed combined with obedience to hand and leg, no reference is made to the speed obtained for trotting matches, which is done by making the horse throw his weight forward and bore on the hand.

A horse out of hand, when trotting fast, seldom moves evenly with his hind-legs; he struggles and drags them after the fore. We should find it very difficult to hold such a horse together but a horse that had been properly reined in would be easily managed; the hand would bring his head home, while the pressure of the legs brought his hind quarters under him, and thus we should maintain his balance, while the limbs in action passed from the bend to the extension before the weight of the body required their support.

Canter is a repetition of bounds, during which the forehand rises first, and higher than the hindquarters. The horse being properly placed, light in hand and well balanced, throw his weight from the forehand to the haunches (by increasing the pressure of the legs and restraining him with the reins) and according to the hand you wish to strike off to, throw the weight of the horse to the opposite side; that is, if he is to lead off with the off fore, followed by off hind (or canter to the right on the circle), throw the weight to his near side, principally upon the left hind-leg, and thus almost fix it to the ground. This is done by feeling both reins to the left, and closing the right leg; the horse's head remains placed to the right, and the left leg merely prevents him from throwing out his haunches. The horse's off legs are thus at liberty, and the forward impulse obliges him to use them; at least he could not do otherwise without difficulty.

When speaking of feeling both reins to the left, the horse's head bent to the right, it is not to turn the horse's head to the left, but to bring his weight to the near side.

Captain Louis Nolan, 1852

A horse may canter false, disunited with the fore or disunited with the hind legs. Cantering to the right on a circle:

1. If the horse leads with his left fore followed by his left hind leg, he is cantering false.

2. He is disunited with the fore, if leading with the left fore followed by the right hind leg.

3. And disunited with the hind-legs, if leading with the right fore the right hind leg remains further back than the left one.

In these three cases, the horse when he struck off was not properly placed and well balanced.

In the first instance, he could only have succeeded in striking off to the left by first throwing his weight on to the right legs; to rectify this, feel both reins to the left (horse's head remains placed to the right), to throw the weight to the horse's left side, and, at the same time, close the left leg to bring his haunches in.

In the second instance, when the horse struck off, too

much weight was thrown on the right foreleg; to rectify this, throw the weight of the horse from the forehand to the haunches (by restraining him with the reins). At the same time, feel both reins to the left to relieve the weight from the right foreleg, and close the right leg to keep the horse's haunches steady.

In the third instance, when the horse struck off, too much weight was thrown on the right hind leg. To rectify this, throw the weight of the horse from the haunches to the forehand (by the pressure of the legs), close the left leg more than the right, and at the same time keep the forehand steady with the reins.

In these instances, take a good hold of your horse's head, though without allowing him to bore on your hand; otherwise the leg only communicates a forward impulse, and thus the effect on the hind-quarter is lost.

Always place your horse properly and have him well balanced before you strike him off. Teach him to strike off to the right; on the circle first, then on the straight line. Then teach him the same to the left; and after that, try him at changing leg.

Captain Louis Nolan, 1852

If only it were that simple, Captain Nolan (Number Two in the TREC, Fastest Walk).

Merlin now had to turn and go back over the same course, but walking as quickly as possible, also for up to 30 points. In either of these tests, breaking gait into a trot would give a zero score.

Karen pronounced herself 'happy' with Merlin.

Phase Two – Obstacles (Part 1, the Rein Back). Four blocks

were placed on the ground as the corners of a rectangle. Competitors had to walk into the rectangle and halt with the horse's front hooves parallel with the two further blocks, then rein back four paces, and walk forward out of the rectangle.

Points up to 10 were awarded for 'calmness, straightness, obedience and regularity of quality of the pace'; also for rider's correct positioning and use of aids (legs and hands). Karen thought Merlin did well at this too, but how would he cope with the maypole?

This is a difficult one. Horse and rider have to circle a pole, connected to it by a rope that the rider holds in one hand. Depending on how confident the rider feels, and how competitive instincts are tempered by feelings of playing safe, the choice is made between walking (up to 5 points), trotting (up to 10) and cantering (up to 15).

Cones mark the course, with a stick in the ground where the rope is attached. Karen and Merlin walked; Karen picked up the rope, kept to the walk correctly around the pole to the next cone, stopped and replaced the rope.

Points were awarded for calmness of horse and rider and accuracy in the exercise. If the rope was dropped or the maypole pulled over, this would be a zero score. Points were deducted for not achieving the chosen pace by the second cone – this didn't apply as Merlin was walking – and for not keeping to the pace all the way around the circle – that was fine, and for the rider holding his hands up too high. Karen could not be accused of that: her hands were too low and so the fourth kind of penalty was incurred: for allowing the rope to touch the ground.

'Merlin is normally good at this exercise but we couldn't keep the rope tight. Rider error. Not good,' she explained.

Number 3 is simply titled Steps, which doesn't really do it justice. At the top of the show ground, tall twin hedges of cypress have been grown, maybe five metres high, two metres apart, with a flight of wooden steps between. Horse and rider have to go up the steps and down the other side. From the horse's point of view the disturbing thing is the darkness, especially on a sunny day such as this, with deep black shadows in stark contrast to the brightly lit world outside the staircase.

One of the competitors would not go in and up. His rider tried several times, at a slow walk, at a quick walk, coming at it from a distance, but no. As soon as the pairing reached the entrance to the black hole, the horse stopped dead and would not move forward at any price. Rather, he wanted to turn around, and so lurched into the cypress trees on his left side. This was exactly what Merlin had done two years before, when he tried it in training.

Up to 10 points would be awarded for calmness and balance of the horse and good position of the rider. Points would be deducted for a break in forward movement or a change in gait from a walk. Completing the majority of the obstacle in a gait other than a walk would result in a zero score – so no cantering up the steps, then.

Merlin and Karen approached the black hole calmly. Reaching the bottom step, was that a slight hesitation, and a little lurch to the side? Yes, it was, but only a slight one. Onwards and upwards.

At the far end of the steps was a gate, test number 4 of the obstacles. Quite a solid gate, and high enough to be easily reached by the riders without over-stretching, it had to be opened by hand only, kept in the grip as the pairing rode through, and closed by hand alone. Points would be awarded for calmness and obedience of the horse, appropriate skills shown by the rider, and for keeping hold of the gate. Points would be deducted for the rider letting go of the gate, allowing a loose gate to touch the horse, or for the horse pushing the gate.

Oh dear. 'Had to let go, I'm afraid. Supposed to keep your hands on it all the time,' Karen explained.

Now the ditch, number 5: no fence, just a ditch. No animal likes to cross over holes in the ground – that's why cattle grids work. This one could be done at a walk (up to 5 points), trot (10 points) or canter (15 points). Karen, playing safe again, elected to walk it. Points would be awarded for calmness, balance and impulsion, and correct posture. Changes in gait or hesitation would be penalised, and a complete refusal would get zero. 'I'll give it five,' said Karen afterwards.

Number 6 is called Immobility, and it happens inside the circular stockade used for outdoor lunging. This is where, normally, in training, the human stands in the middle and on the end of a rope the horse runs round and round. All the horses in this event had been in here, in the lunge pen, dozens of times. Today, though, things would be different. For a start there was a circle of rope laid out on the ground, and a mounting block.

Competitors are to ride their horses into the lunge pen and into the rope circle, and halt. Dismount. Run the stirrup irons up on both sides, twist the reins and secure using the throat lash. Leave the horse in the centre of the circle, walk out and stand next to the mounting block. Time allowed so far: one minute.

That done, the stopwatch is started. The horse is to stand

still in the rope circle for 30 seconds (only verbal commands may be used by the rider). The judge will stop the watch if so much as a hoof is seen outside the rope. One point will be awarded for every three seconds the horse stands inside the circle, and one point deducted for every ten seconds taken over the initial minute allowance.

Well, the first minute was fine, wasn't it, Karen and Merlin? And then what happened?

Merlin ticked up three points for standing still for ten seconds, then he remembered what he used to do in here, in this pen, all that time ago when he was a callow youth, learning to be a police horse. This was where Jo Sullivan used to bring him, and have him trotting and cantering round and round. There was no lunge rope now, but never mind, he would do without it; he would do some self-lunging, and off he went at a fast trot, anti-clockwise, head down until he reached the point where he could glance over the fence at the other horses, and round and round again.

There were several minutes of this fun before a slightly irate Karen could catch Merlin, calm him down and lead him to the next test: number 7, Mounting. This was just a question of undoing the stirrups and reins and getting on the damn horse at the mounting block. Points would be awarded for calmness and obedience of the horse. Huh. And correct mounting procedure of the rider. Quite.

You have one minute to complete the mounting; penalty points will be awarded once the time has elapsed. No problem, and Merlin had already forgotten all about lunging himself – 'Once mounted, we'll ride out of here and go and stand in the shade, under that tree over there, ready for the next test. While I'm waiting, I'll just have a little munch on these leaves. *Very* tasty.'

The next test, number 8, was the Canter Corridor. The corridor in question was made up of poles, four of them, laid in parallel pairs on the ground, 80 centimetres apart. Up to 10 points would be awarded for approach and accuracy through the poles, and penalty points would be incurred for the horse touching the poles. If the horse fails to stay within the poles for the full duration of the exercise, the competitor scores zero.

The trick here is for horse and rider to look straight ahead and not at the poles.

Your worships, the witness states that the judge on this event had failed to notice that the poles had not been relaid in exact parallel after the previous competitor had disturbed them. They were laid in V shapes, making a narrow kind of waistline in the middle. Therefore, it was not Merlin's fault that he kicked them out of the way as he cantered through; we demand a recount.

Fat chance. On to number 9 and the last test, The Weave – a slalom through a line of five traffic cones at the walk, trot or canter. Karen chose to trot. Points will be awarded for smoothness and accuracy. Merlin, that was perfect. Ten points, surely? But, we have to say, not much hope of a silver cup for Best Trained Horse, not with all that self-lunging, and the slack rope round the maypole, and the letting go of the gate, and the break from slow canter.

Ah well, it's the taking part that matters, not the winning. In any case, as PC Howell put it: as usually happens Imber Court win everything, and they won this too. Merlin, alas, did not have one of his best days. He did even worse than the previous time when, as a very fresh freshman, newly out of school, he came 6th out of 20.

Today, we are sorry to say, Merlin was adjudged 12th out of

16. The stock response from police officers is that being good at maypoles and traffic-cone slaloms doesn't necessarily match up with being good at controlling crowds and leading regimental bands. So there.

How do you train a horse to jump through a flaming hoop? Gradually, of course, starting with straight jumps over the wooden base, then adding the heavy metal hexagonal hoop. Then have a little fire and smoke at the base of the hoop and have the horse go round the outside of it, and so on. The hoop has a groove in it, so they lay that on the ground, pour petrol in the groove, set it up and light it, and it burns long enough for all the horses in the Activity Ride (eight of them) to jump through several times. No problem at all.

The finale of the Ride, which is the finale of the Noel McCarthy Day, is for one horse to canter right down and over the line of bush jumps, with a very special jump at the end. This has a different sort of hoop fitted, one completely covered in white paper. Jumping through a blank sheet is not something they all train to do as it takes such a lot of time and effort, so one horse is nominated as 'Paper Breaker'. Remember, the horse is being asked to trust his rider so entirely and so unquestioningly that he will jump through a wall. We know it's paper; to the horse, it's solid – it could be painted brick.

The horse is introduced to the idea by having an enormous sheet of paper draped around his neck while he is ridden around. Once he's happy with that, he'll be shown a partly papered hoop, with a large gap in it. This is similar in the horse's mind to his first jump training, where he sees a jump with 'wings' on either side, which are gradually narrowed until going through to the jump is the only option.

The gap in the paper gets smaller and smaller, until the big day when he's asked to jump through a white, opaque disk with no knowledge of what's on the other side. You may not be able to make a horse drink when you take him to water, but you can train him to have such total trust in his partner that he'll go through a wall for you.

All the horses in the Activity Ride today are new to the game. They've trained for a fortnight in cavalry manoeuvres with a difference – lots of charging about in lines, wheeling, jumping, but criss-crossing in patterns and passing each other in opposite directions. Four horses head for a jump left to right, while the other four head for the same jump, right to left. Timing is everything.

And here they come, walking slowly in single file up the parade ground, beside the white picket fence. In front is Inspector Russell Pickin on Lochearn. Second is Merlin, ridden by Sergeant Craig Richards. Inspector Pickin stops, and they all stop. Merlin stands like a statue, while Lochearn does a little jig on the spot. They're waiting, eager to start, and off they go at a slow canter, eight horses, seemingly arranged according to size and colour, with the two smaller, darker ones at the back, and the four lighter bays in the middle.

They wheel gently to the left, keeping almost perfectly equal distance between each other, and turn more sharply left again to line up the row of six bush jumps, which they take at a quicker canter. At the end of the line they split. Lochearn peels off to the right, Merlin to the left, and the others follow alternately.

Wheeling around to meet again at the top of the jump line, they head for it in pairs, Lochearn and Merlin in the lead. They jump the first fence not quite in harmony. Merlin is in front by a nose and two legs, and again at the second. The third is jumped almost together, and the fourth is spot on. Sergeant Richards had a bit of persuasion to do there: that Merlin, he will want to be in front.

Oh, something's gone wrong. After three pairs have jumped together, one horse jumps on his own. Oh, maybe it's not wrong. The non-runner is standing beside the fence, waiting. Merlin and Lochearn peel off again in opposite directions, ride up the field to the top of the jump line, and the standing horse moves forward to join them; they go down the line of jumps as a trio, with the new friend in the middle.

They jump all the fences in near-perfect unison. That was good. There is only just enough room on the fence for three horses abreast and they have to ride very close together. Merlin and friend peel off to their left, Lochearn to the right. The second three do the same, and the final pair split each way.

The men on the ground, the helpers, are led by legendary trainer Alistair Blamire and include Merlin's next partner, Jecks Hyde. They rush around frantically, moving pieces of jump about. They're making a pattern of half-width brush fences, two rows of two at 90 degrees, making a sort of open square. And now the horses come at it from east and south, as it were, jumping in turns, crossing each other's paths with only instants to spare.

And they do it again, coming the other way. Crikey, that was a close one. Nose and tail made contact. Oh, and there's a fence down. A helper leaps to put it up again. These are not tall fences, not show jumping heights, just below the belly line on the horses so they shouldn't really knock one over. Perhaps some of the crowd didn't notice. Most of them did, seeing as they're all in the business.

What's happening now? They're wheeling about in a complicated way, heading for the top of the field, while one horse remains standing at the bottom. Here comes Merlin, with Lochearn again, and they jump down the line that the boys have reassembled, in a pair as before. Hey, wait a minute! That standing horse, he's heading at the line of jumps in the opposite direction. He's going to jump in between Merlin and Lochearn.

Merlin keeps going, but Lochearn veers away a little. Oh my goodness, what confusion. Some have kept going but one has refused, wanting to go early through one of the hoops, and lost his rider. Is that the inspector? No, it isn't, but as it was the fault of the horse in front, in the wrong place, forcing a sharp swerve, we shall not say who it was. Another horse has charged into one of the box fences used to hold up the hoops. It's not quite chaos but, in contrast to the precision and timing we've seen so far, it's certainly verging on it.

The team needs a leader. After a little hesitation, they reform the line behind Merlin and canter around in a big circle and away back to the top of the field while the helpers put up another jump crossways.

One line of four canters down the jump line while the others, led by Merlin, go round in a half circle and begin their jumps west to east while the first line jumps north to south. They're criss-crossing again, very close to each other, and very impressive it is.

Circling, they reform into a line of seven – one is standing still, waiting for something – and canter down the line of jumps, with Merlin at the front. At the end they split, left and right, and head for the arrangement of hoops forming an open square. They jump through these, crossing each other's paths, while the helpers scurry about doing something or other – ah, they have flaming torches. While the horses circle, they light the hoops. At first the flames burn slowly, then spread all the way around the hoops, making smoke and leaving only enough flame-free space in the centre of the hoop for a horse to get through.

At this, the helpers run clear and crouch down. The flames are really going now, and the wind takes the fire and the smoke across the hoops. With no hesitation whatsoever, the riders take their horses through the flames, through the hoops, criss-crossing with immaculate timing, and they do so again.

Sergeant Richards waves a signal and they head away to the top of the field once more and canter down the bush jumps, Merlin in the lead, the officers taking off their uniform jackets as they do so. Look Mum, no hands.

Round they go, Merlin still at the front, and they come down the jumps, putting their jackets back on. No hands again. Some have a bit of bother jumping and fastening buttons at the same time, but most of them manage it. One horse decides to go round a jump rather than over, but otherwise a neat manoeuvre.

Now we find out why that horse has been waiting. As soon as the last jacket putter-onner is clear, two helpers run to the end of the jump line and hold up the hoop covered in paper as the waiting horse begins his approach. Looking from the bottom of the field, all that can be seen is the wall of white paper. A couple of seconds pass, and the horse and rider burst through, setting off a firework shower.

The last officer gets his jacket back on, and Merlin leads the line up to the jumps, with the riders holding their stirrups out wide in their hands. Look, Mum, no legs.

Oh no, two of the riders are still fiddling with their jackets. More rehearsal required on that one. Maybe they should have Velcro.

Big circle again, and they're all riding on left rein while the right hand is on the saddle. Ah, they've taken their saddles out from under them, all except Inspector Pickin, leading the line but perhaps still recovering from his paper breaking. They take the jumps, waving their saddles in the air, and come to the bottom of the field, where they form a line abreast and take their bow. Exeunt stage right, bareback, in half section. Brilliant, terrific! And encore in pairs again, waving their saddles.

'The Mounted Unit officer is the Department's "Ambassador of Goodwill" and will strive to leave each citizen contacted with a positive impression of the MU specifically, and the Department in general.'

San Jose Police Department Special Operations
Procedure Manual

When San Jose's Cinco de Mayo festival ended at about 5.30pm, groups of people, allegedly from rival gangs, gathered on Santa Clara Street. Not wanting to start trouble, the mounted officers held back. By the time action looked like becoming necessary, the crowd felt itself to be in possession of the street.

A young man was hit with a bottle and knocked unconscious. More people began to throw bottles. The police started a sweep, with a line of officers on foot and on motorcycles attempting to move the crowd of over 2,000 down Santa Clara Street. The rioters surged forward and the Mounted Unit moved in, through a hail of flying bottles, garbage bins and any bits of street furniture that could be broken and thrown.

It took the Mounted Unit only 15 minutes to disperse the crowd. 'The horses are very effective at calming people down,' Sergeant Urban explained. 'It's sobering. I think that's the best word I can use to describe the feeling of having horses coming at you – everything in your body tells you it's time to go.'

None of the police horses hesitated before plunging into the melee. 'They really showed how courageous they were that day,' Urban added. 'We train intensely and it really paid off, because none of those horses were freaking out. The funny thing was, when we got done dispersing the rioters and the looters, 15 minutes later we were riding back through the downtown and little kids were saying, "Got any stickers? Got any cards?" Here, the horses were still kind of agitated and everybody was still pumped up, and the little kids were like the Pied Pipers walking down the street.'

Three women of Middletown, Providence, Rhode Island were charged with cruelty to animals after they assaulted a patrolman's horse.

The incident occurred when a mounted patrolman was trying to clear the crowd of people spilling out of downtown clubs. A woman started petting the horse but then her companion, Karyn Schiliro, 21, hit the mare so hard in the rear that the animal kicked out, almost striking two passers-by. When the patrolman threatened to arrest Schiliro, the young woman just laughed and hit the horse again. Then another woman, Lindsay Kircher, 21, hit the horse with a pizza box and a third woman, Tammy Polley, 20, hit the horse on the head with a soda can. After a short chase, the mounted patrolman and another officer caught the women and arrested them. The horse, named Fleet, was not seriously hurt.

In Hyderabad in 2001, a demonstration organised to protest against alleged irregularities in electricity bills proved fatal to a police horse in a freak accident. Hundreds of Congress party workers had gathered at the State power company's headquarters to protest against increases in prices and wrong billings. The city police made elaborate arrangements for maintaining law and order during the agitation and deployed 10 Mounted Police to control the crowd.

The 10 horses were taken inside the company's gates and kept in a state of readiness without realising that they were standing close to the generator room. All hell broke loose when power failed in the buildings and an electrician started the generator.

Made to panic by the loud sound of the generator coming from behind, the horses ran amuck. Some of them fell on the ground and Bahadur, a black horse, hit a boulder and collapsed on the spot. 'It could have either broken its neck or taken the impact of the fall on the head, which caused its death,' a company official observed.

Mr K Jagannath Rao, Additional Superintendent of Police, said the exact cause of Bahadur's death was yet to be confirmed. 'We have also checked the place to rule out the possibility of the horse dying due to electrocution,' he said.

Later, the Joint Commissioner, Dr B L Meena, inspected the premises where the horse died. 'We have ordered the autopsy of the horse. A government veterinary doctor is already seized with the matter and we would know the exact cause of death by night,' he said. According to officials, Bahadur was one of the horses recently brought from Dubai.

July 2013, Austin, Texas: A man was arrested early Sunday after he burned a police horse with a cigarette after the bars had closed, according to an arrest affidavit. At about 2.45am, police responded to an incident on East Sixth Street, near San Jacinto Boulevard, where a woman was arrested. A crowd became upset and the mounted patrol attempted to control it.

An officer said he saw a man, later identified as 23-year-old Tyrone Branch Jr, take a lit cigarette and burn the right side of his police horse, Drago, between the neck and head. The horse moved his head violently, the affidavit said.

'If the horse rears up, the officer can only do so much to control a large animal like that,' said police Sergeant David Daniels, a spokesman for the department. 'If the horse falls on somebody, that would be a bad situation.'

In the affidavit police stated that Drago had a small burn mark that appeared fresh.

'An officer's horse is an extension of the police family,' Daniels declared.

Branch was arrested at the scene and charged with

interference with a police service animal, a state jail felony punishable by up to two years. His bail was set at $8,000.

In July 2013, it was announced that police horses were to be used in Bristol and Somerset in a bid to engage with the community and reduce anti-social behaviour and low-level crime.

Avon and Somerset is the only police force in the West Country with a Mounted section. However, this would be the first time for them to be deployed in local estates.

'The idea came about because in the school holidays there is an increase in anti-social behaviour and we thought about what we could do to cut this,' explained PC Ted Grabowski. 'We are not saying that areas like Southmead and Hartcliffe are really bad but anti-social behaviour and low-level crime do tend to go up on these estates when the children break up from school. I think there are several factors. Boredom is one, and their general inquisitiveness can sometimes lead to them doing something they should not.'

By policing on horseback, the Force would be able to get to areas that cars cannot reach, and interact with local residents who are more likely to approach the horses.

'We are hoping that by bringing the horses, people will come up to us and we will be able to talk to them, engage them and build up a relationship with the community,' continued PC Grabowski. 'We hope our presence on the streets will also provide reassurance to the community in general. Hopefully, it will create a better atmosphere for the adult residents as well as the children.'

Pairs of Mounted Police would patrol Southmead and Hartcliffe in Bristol, and Bridgwater in Somerset, a few times a week. If the pilot project was successful, it would be extended to other areas during school holidays.

Chapter Eight

Where Do We Go From Here?

Inspector Danny Butler used to be the training manager at Imber Court. In his many years of Mounted Police service, as PC, sergeant and now inspector, he's seen massive changes.

'When I started, in 1991, we had 19 operational stables around the Metropolitan area, now we have 7. We had 200 horses – in fact, 201, I recall – and we're now down to just over 100. So we've halved in strength in my time, but I would say we're doing about three times the amount of work. I can show you what that means.

'In my early days, we had maybe a dozen horses around 25 years old, and we'd had them since they went into training when they were just three or four. I can only think of one in the last five years that's reached such an age while still on duty – we have to retire them so much earlier.

'Football is a prime example; we have a lot more of it. Television sets the agenda for the Premier League, and there's a lot more European football than there used to be, and so now we can have games on any and every day of the week, and almost right through the year. Football season? There's no such thing now. It can happen that an individual officer and horse team could be going to the football five days in one week; it does happen. And they're long, long days. And you might be able to point to a few days in June when there isn't any football.

'The role has changed too. In the old days the job was public order, now it's more oriented towards public safety. The segregation of fans is much better now, better planned, better co-ordinated, so we're less likely to have a punch-up to deal with. It's more scientific, if you like. We manage crowd dynamics. Compared to what there was in the late eighties and early nineties, we don't have anything like as much disorder now because we are better at the job.

'This is not to say the problem has disappeared. If we took our eye off the ball, as it were, it could all start up again. There are still the significant numbers of people who don't really come to the match for the football. These are people looking for trouble and they align themselves with a football club in the hope of finding it. They need policing, and we are there to do that. We are the insurance policy against violence.

'Take the Champions League Final at Wembley [in May 2013]. Two German teams, Bayern Munich and Borussia Dortmund, with many thousands of travelling fans each, and they do things differently. These are the mums and dads, the kids, the dedicated fans, the occasional fans, the ultras and the hooligans, and they all gather en masse before the game at a place away from the ground, and they march all together to the ground.

'This is what happened with Bayern Munich. They all pitched up and assembled in a park near Wembley, and marched through the streets: 10,000 people. That's a lot of people in one group, tramping through the streets of northwest London, a foreign country to them, and who would know what was going to happen? The Dortmund lot did much the same, collecting together and marching on the stadium, and before we got there, when there were only foot police and not many of them, coaches were attacked and quite a serious incident blew up.

'We knew they would do the marching. We were used to it, but when they came to a London club in one of the rounds, there was nothing like so many: maybe 3,000, which we can manage reasonably comfortably – but 10,000? Even with the vast majority in good spirits and there for a great occasion, that's a lot, and it requires more police horses than any domestic match. You could have Arsenal and Spurs in the Cup Final at Wembley and we wouldn't need so many, because the supporters come in small quantities, dribs and drabs. Yes, you will have some bigger groups, especially what we call the risk supporters, the ones out for trouble; they tend to stick together. But you're talking dozens and scores, maybe a couple of hundred at the most. But 10,000, wow!

'They came with their own police spotting teams, as happens everywhere now with football. Any police district, anywhere in Europe that has a football club within the boundaries, will have some sort of liaison, some sort of dedicated football police activity, and, with the bigger clubs in terms of support, the fans' organisations will field their own stewards to work with the police.

'Anyway, when the crowds saw the mounted officers and we asked them to move along, even though we were so outnumbered, they did as requested, good as gold.'

We are reminded of the time in a modest Lancashire town one Saturday morning, when the Secretary of Accrington Stanley rang the Duty Inspector about policing for that afternoon's game (mounted officers were not an option). 'How many do you want?' asked the Inspector. 'One,' said the Secretary. 'One?' asked the Inspector. 'Yes, it's all we can afford,' said the Secretary. 'I'll send four,' said the Inspector, 'but make sure you let them in for nothing.'

If football is a major part of Mounted life in London's police, the other aspect that is outside normal police work is the ceremonial duty, for Merlin and Great Scotland Yard and Hyde Park stations at any rate. Surely the Changing of the Guard and all that couldn't happen without the Mounted Branch?

Inspector Danny Butler: 'Well, I'm not so sure. There is a school of thought that says we could do it another way. Who's to say we couldn't do it with bobbies on bicycles, two by two? The tourists wouldn't be quite so impressed, but who's paying here? Are we doing it for the tourists, or are we looking at simple, practical policing that states we must choose the most cost-effective option?

'Admittedly, the Met is in a unique position as regards Mounted Branch, but even we are under pressure to do things differently. If someone says, what are we doing with horses in the twenty-first century, how do we answer? If someone says, how many of your 105 horses are capable of doing all the various jobs, and you have to answer they're all good at most things but the Merlins that can do anything, well, say, about 65. So the bean counters say, get rid of the other 40. Which would mean, for the 65 all-rounders, not three times the work of the old days, but four times, and even shorter working lives for the animals.'

The non-horsey person, imagining the aforementioned plough horse plodding his weary way up and down the field all day long, or the recreational animal walking the bridleways of the Yorkshire Dales, can take this early retirement as proof of the physical and mental strain the police horse must bear.

Danny Butler: 'They're in a completely alien environment. You could say they should be in a meadow somewhere, head down, munching the green grass, but instead we're asking them to do a job of work that's foreign to their nature. We're putting them under pressure, and we're putting their bodies, their limbs, to the test six days a week. The streets of London are not paved with gold, they're paved with concrete, and that is hard on a horse.'

It's a circular argument. If you have horses, you must allow for them being horses and not motorcycles. Are the bean counters going to have so much sway that a police officer on a pedal bike will be directing traffic at the Trooping of the Colour? And what will happen at the major demonstrations?

Danny Butler: 'As we speak, we're planning for a big march by the EDL, the English Defence League. We'll be able to put out 40 horses or more for that. I can't see we'd be able to manage more than that, but there are plenty of arguments that we should have more. More cuts, fewer horses, less ability to manage things like that.

'Essex police always had a Mounted section, then they disbanded it, and the Chief Constable resurrected it in 2005. We went up there, trained them, helped them with buying horses, advised them on the set-up, and now they've closed it again. When he restarted it, the Chief Constable said it was in response to public demand but when the chips are down and cost-cuts have to be made, the Mounted section is a soft option.'

Essex, however, does not have the Houses of Parliament, focus for all demos against government policy, nor does it have all the foreign embassies, again the targets for demos against policies and events abroad. London has an enormous and extremely diverse population, and it's easy to get to when you want even more people on your march. The city will always be the capital of political protest, and police officers on bicycles simply would not be up to the job.

Generally, marches and demonstrations are not mounted by those with middle-of-the-road opinions; they tend to be concerned with core issues or even extreme views – which generate agitation among those opposing the views – or with heartfelt, emotionally charged matters such as the Poll Tax, the Criminal Justice Bill, the Countryside Alliance march for 'Liberty and Livelihood' of 2002, the Iraq War, or the 2009 G20 summit. All these crowd-events must have starts and finishes, where large numbers can assemble. Lately added to the conventional big demos along the usual routes to Trafalgar Square and Westminster are the smaller ones that can be equally disruptive when they take several different routes from less popular points. One, for instance, began at Liverpool Street station and set off in five directions.

It's very difficult to see how London could cope without the Mounted Police.

Police horses want for nothing in terms of food and shelter, healthcare of the very best, and they're working with people who love and look after them. You can't say it was what they were made for, or what they evolved to be, but they don't complain, bless them.

So, what will happen next? Police and Crime Commissioners and senior police officers are having to look at Force collaboration and the possibility of regional Mounted Units as a way of operating Mounted Police in the future in Great Britain. In recent times, as forces have come under heavier financial pressure, numbers of Mounted Units have declined from 17 to 14 to 12, including the amalgamation of the two in Scotland into a single Mounted Branch in Strathclyde.

South Yorkshire Police's Mounted section was due to be merged with those of the West Yorkshire and Humberside Forces, but Humberside instead disbanded its unit altogether. The merger plan has also been dropped, replaced by a collaboration agreement between the West and South Forces.

The Police and Crime Commissioner for South Yorkshire, Mr Shaun Wright, said: 'In these times of austerity, savings have been made. I am confident that the Mounted section will still be able to maintain its high visibility and help keep South Yorkshire's streets safe with the savings we have introduced.'

Twelve constables in the South Yorkshire unit are to become eight, with the six support staff reduced to four. Two of the current 12 horses are set to retire and will not be replaced. If special circumstances demand more Mounted resources, West Yorkshire will step in.

In June 2012, Nottinghamshire Police announced it would close its Mounted section to save £93,000. Officers and support staff were reassigned; four of the horses were retired and the rest transferred to other forces (Greater Manchester, South Wales and City of London).

Three months later, the Nottinghamshire Police and Crime Commissioner, fulfilling an election promise, announced the possibility of setting it up again, although the loss of the unit had, apparently, not been painfully felt. Or, as a spokesperson put it, 'Comprehensive analysis and a consultation process were undertaken before a final decision was made. Resource-intensive events have occurred, but police horses have not been required.'

While other forces reduce or disband their Mounted Units, Avon and Somerset Police is planning an increase from 10 horses to 15. A senior officer said: 'They are useful at both ends of the policing spectrum, for community engagement and public order.'

Metropolitan Police Sergeant Paul McKeever, who is chairman of the Police Federation of England and Wales, expressed similar views, in that forces would not be making these cuts without the budgetary pressures because Mounted sections are invaluable in many difficult situations. He said: 'Many police officers will tell you that in public order situations they are priceless. To do the job of one or two police horses, you would need a lot of officers on foot. They are hugely beneficial for crowd control, keeping order and dealing with disorder. One ray of sunshine is that the Met Police are keeping their Mounted numbers up because our commissioner understands they are worth a great deal.'

In the spring of 2012, Operation Trafalgar, in London's West End, aimed to reduce robbery, violent crime, vehicle crime and sex crime, as well as anti-social behaviour, by significant amounts, aided by the Met's biggest deployment of mounted officers outside of public-order duties.

Mounted Branch Inspector Russell Pickin said: 'We are going for high impact, with 32 horses on patrol during Thursday, Friday and Saturday nights, joining the regular and extra Trafalgar officers in Westminster to provide a highly visible and approachable presence. The end of the football season has allowed us to reallocate horses from all over the Met area.'

Operation Trafalgar resulted in hundreds more arrests compared with a normal year. One new ingredient was the police's own form of demonstration, a show of force, staging most of its briefings on the street to reassure the public. More Mounted Branch officers were brought in on 'high impact' days.

Karen Howell: 'Merlin and I attended the first briefing, in Trafalgar Square, along with about 20 other horses and various foot-duty serials. We were all briefed together by a senior officer, with the press present. We then went out in pairs, with each pair being given a designated area of a few streets. Our objective was to provide a high-visibility reassurance patrol and to stop and deal with any crime or anti-social behaviour that we came across.

'From Merlin's point of view, it was riding around, stopping and meeting people, which is what he loves doing. As usual, he behaved very well when I stopped someone, although he was inclined to try and help me by searching through bags and whatnot. He seems to have a nose for people who are up to no good. He's nice as pie with the normal public, but he can be a bit authoritative when we meet somebody who's not so pleasant.'

Good old Merlin. Here's wishing him a long and happy life.

Seven police horses, weighing a total of 5,180 kilos, were weighed at the Ford Engine Plant in Bridgend, South Wales as part of their regular health check.

'The Ford site at Waterton has the only certified weighbridge in the local area, so we've been taking the horses there for years,' explained PC Rick Lewis from the Mounted section at South Wales Police HQ in Bridgend.

'If we couldn't use the weighbridge at Ford, then we'd probably have to transport the horses in a lorry to the nearest quarry, but with Ford being permanently manned and just around the corner, it's convenient for everyone and we can patrol the local area at the same time. We're very grateful to Ford for accommodating us all these years free of charge.'

Inspector Tracy Day of Bedfordshire Police won two competitions in the Blue Lights Horse of the Year Show held at Aintree Racecourse. Inspector Day (39) rode her horse Carrello to victory in the Novice Dressage and the Combined Training (Novice) competition (a mix of dressage and show jumping). She was pipped for top place in the Elementary Dressage by just two points. Riders from Blue Light services around Europe took part in the show, which ran over three days.

Inspector Day said: 'Everyone was really friendly and the event was good fun. To compete in my uniform on behalf of Bedfordshire Police was a real privilege and I felt very proud to have done so. Winning was a bonus and to be presented with prizes in a huge arena in front of hundreds of people was an amazing experience. I was particularly pleased because I won against the German competitors, who are renowned for their dressage talent.'

The Blue Lights Horse of the Year Show is a unique event created and supported by the Police, Fire and Ambulance services in Merseyside, and held at the Aintree International Equestrian Centre.

Mounted Police in London – A Short History

'The Provost must have a horse allowed him and some soldiers to attend him and all the rest commanded to obey and assist, or else the Service will suffer, for he is but one man and must correct many and therefore he cannot be beloved.'

King Charles I, 1629

In May 2012, the municipal police of Mâcon launched their new Mounted Branch (Brigade Équestre). Patrols would operate in districts according to priorities of crime prevention. This has come about due to the enthusiasm of the Mayor, Jean-Patrick Courtois, and henceforth there will be three officers qualified to ride the three horses, covering all the main streets of the town centre, as well as the suburbs.

Said the Mayor: 'I wanted the *Brigade Équestre* because Mâcon is a town where the horse counts for a lot, certainly, but above all I consider it an essential means of crime prevention. This will be a complementary resource with a mission of watchful guardianship, but equally with a charge to reassure and inform the population. Results of experiments have confirmed the positive attractions of the Force, for example in maintaining order and respect for other people and property among the youth.'

'The example of the Mounted Police of Montélimar shows how we can satisfy the wishes of our elected representatives,' said Gérard Gronfier, the Senior Officer of the Municipal Police. 'The Brigade will help to ensure safety at large public assemblies, and expects to be able to improve the civility and citizenship of all.'

As long as there have been established civilised states with citizens hoping to live in peace and liberty, so there have been police forces of one kind or another. Our word 'police' comes from Greek and Latin roots meaning 'the state' and 'citizenship', and to the police has been entrusted the duty of maintaining public order among the citizens and enforcing the State's regulations for the common good.

The definition of public order and the types of regulations to be enforced have changed considerably since the Ancient Egyptians, the Romans, the Normans and others set up their 'police' forces, not always with the common good as top priority. In the 13th century Edward I of England made a law that strict watch should be kept in London 'by strong men with good arms', while, nearly 400 years later, Charles I may well have been the first king to specify the use of mounted strongmen to perform this task, although it is not known how well they did it.

Many Acts of Parliament later, at the beginning of the 18th century, there was still no properly organised police force as we might recognise it, in London or anywhere else in Britain, but the need for it was beyond doubt. Travelling along the roads, such as they were, leading into the towns was an extremely dangerous undertaking, with robbers and highwaymen lurking at every likely corner, while the streets of the towns themselves were similarly infested with footpads and muggers (footpads were highwaymen who worked on foot, rather than on horseback).

The problem, naturally enough, was at its worst in the biggest town. There was a system of watchmen in some London parishes but the watchers were poorly paid. As you might expect, they, and the similarly low-paid constables, who acted as enforcers for the Justices of the Peace, were unreliable and bribable, and liable to spend their time in the local alehouse rather than putting themselves in danger by making a fuss among the criminal classes or disturbing their places of resort.

But things were about to change. In 1739, the Commissioner for the Peace in the county of Middlesex and the City of Westminster, Sir Thomas de Veil, moved his office – and so his court – to a house in Bow Street. He was a vigorous enforcer of the Law and personally courageous. Having sorted out his constables, firing and hiring, he made Bow Street a notable centre of the justice system. Henry Fielding, author of *Tom Jones* (1749), succeeded de Veil in his commissions and his house, was appointed chief magistrate for the metropolis and set the process going that would soon lead to the first modern Mounted Police.

Fielding put together a plan for reforming and reorganising the policing system, which was ignored by the British government. His response was to set up a small group of men of courage and integrity, six of them plus a leader, called 'thief-takers', on a full-time wage of a guinea a week (£1 1s 0d or 105p, roughly double an ordinary labourer's wage of the time and worth several hundred pounds in today's money), plus bounty money if a criminal was successfully prosecuted.

In 1754, Henry's half-brother, Sir John, succeeded him as court justice, in effect the government's adviser on law and order. Sir John had lost his eyesight through an incompetent surgeon at the age of 19 and was subsequently known as 'The Blind Beak', but was said to be able to recognise any of London's 3,000 most persistent criminals by their voices. He set up a system of recording and publishing the details of crimes and criminals to back up his thief-taker/detectives, who by now were known as the Bow Street Runners, and set about tackling the problem of highway robbery on the routes in and out of London.

His first suggestion, that leading citizens should subscribe to a fund for a small force of mounted officers, did not meet with approval, but he did eventually persuade the government to put up the money for a horse patrol in 1763.

The date is significant. There was public alarm at the possibility of a crime wave to follow the great demobilisation of the Army after the Treaty of Paris, signed that year, ended the Seven Years' War. As a result, £600 was assigned to put 10 men on horseback, armed with sword, pistol and truncheon but with no uniform dress, to patrol the London turnpikes as far as six miles from Charing Cross. They went out at night, initially for a six-month experiment, and were very successful indeed. Highway robbery almost disappeared as a threat to travellers but the money ran out after little more than a year and as there was clearly no need for it any more, no further funding was forthcoming. The first metropolitan Mounted Branch, a victim of its own success, was disbanded. At this the highwaymen rejoiced and promptly went back into business.

There had been no suggestion of using Mounted Police to maintain public order, although there was just as serious a need for it as there had been for defeating the highwaymen. Between 1780 and the foundation of the Metropolitan Police in 1829, there were 80 riots in London, small and large, and the Army had to be used in the most serious instances. In the notorious Gordon riots of 1780, a mob attacked the Bow Street court and destroyed Fielding's records, while troops opened fire on rioters storming the Bank of England, killing or wounding some 500 people.

The Middlesex Justices Act of 1792 (Middlesex then corresponding to much of the metropolis, excluding the Cities of London and of Westminster) established seven 'public offices' in addition to Bow Street. In effect, these were combined magistrates' courts and police stations, each having three justices and six constables, all full-time employed and not reliant on rewards, bounties or other kickbacks for a living. By 1797, Bow Street – the Scotland Yard of its day – was operating with 68 patrolling constables, some of whom sometimes went on horseback.

At last, in 1805, under the direction of Sir Richard Ford, Chief Magistrate and Superintendent of Aliens, the Bow

Street Horse Patrol was revived. This time there was no argument about funding although there was still no thought of using the mounted men for crowd control. This was purely an anti-criminal initiative.

Two inspectors and 52 constables were recruited, most of them with army cavalry experience, and they were issued with a uniform, possibly the first police uniform in the world. They wore a long, dark blue coat, top hat and a scarlet waistcoat that is said to have earned them the inevitable 'Robin Redbreast' nickname. The men patrolled right out to Barnet, Epsom, Romford, Enfield, Windsor – all quite separate, independent towns then – on the way to London but not yet part of it. Their watchwords were 'Be Sober. Be Vigilant' and, for the first time, there was clearly an identifiable, highly visible Mounted Police presence in the capital, and its members gave voice to an early form of call sign when challenging anyone: 'Bow Street Patrol.'

In those days, magistrates took a more active part in policing, with powers of arrest they were expected to use frequently. Sir Richard Ford was no backslider in this respect. Highwaymen and robbers, though much reduced in numbers, were still a serious problem, especially where main roads crossed rough country, the commons and heaths – for example, Hounslow Heath, then traversed by the Roman road to Exeter (the Great Western Road, now the A30), off which branched the Oxford and Bath road (now the A4). Brave Sir Richard disguised himself as a much older man and rode alone across the Heath, with members of his horse patrol in hiding. When attacked by footpads, out rode the patrolmen to the rescue and to take up the villains.

At this time, it was estimated that there was one practising criminal for every 22 Londoners. If this figure was correct, there were around 90,000 ne'er-do-wells, mostly thieves, at work in the metropolis, plus the many thousands of vagrants, prostitutes, drunk-and-disorderly characters and beggars who thronged the streets. The small force of professional magistrates and constables established at Bow Street, and elsewhere in London after the 1792 Act, mounted or otherwise, could not be expected to make great inroads into such a total. The ancient system of parish-based beadles, watchmen and part-time semi-voluntary constables could not do much either, and never had. Their authority was often so particularly defined within parish boundaries that a disturbance in the Red Lion on the east side of the street could be dealt with, but not the fight in the White Hart, over on the west side.

There was a crying need for an all-London solution to the problem but in 1812, 1818 and 1822, parliamentary committees appointed to investigate crime and policing were unable to come up with any ideas for reform. Many important people expressed the view that a large, organised and well-structured police force was unconstitutional, would infringe liberties and might even be a government subterfuge to control those in tyranny, like the secret police that some continental countries maintained.

Meanwhile, the Bow Street Horse Patrol carried on, with its rulebook: 'Orders and Directions to be Observed by the Police Horse Patrol.' In the text below, the 1827 version, the word 'patrol' can mean the officer himself as well as his work:

List of Appointments *with which each Horse Patrol is furnished, Severally marked with the Number by which the*

Patrol is designated
Cutlass and Belt
Pistol and Case
Handcuffs, with Key and Case
Truncheon
Book of Orders in Case
The Regulated Uniform *of the Police Horse Patrol is a*
Blue double-breasted Coat, with yellow Metal Buttons
Scarlet Waistcoat
Blue Trowsers [sic]
Wellington Boots
White Neckcloth
Black Felt Hat

The Duty of the Horse Patrol is to afford Protection to Persons travelling on the High Roads, *for which purpose they are to patrol the Roads at such a regular pace as will bring them to the several points on the Road, at the time they are directed.*

Every Patrol is to take particular notice of all Persons of suspicious appearance, whom he may see on the Road, and to pay attention to whatever Information he may receive, of any Highway, or Footpad Robbery, Burglary or other Felony *having been committed, or attempted; or of any suspicious Persons having been seen on the Road; and to endeavour to obtain a description of them, and the Road they may have taken; and if any* Highway or Footpad Robbery, Burglary or other Felony *shall have been committed, or attempted, he is to join the other patrol on the Road, if he can conveniently do so, and then use every exertion to take the Offenders; or if he cannot conveniently join any other Patrol, he is to make an immediate pursuit with such other assistance as he may meet with, and if the Party should be apprehended, to lodge them in some place of security, until he can bring them to the Public Office in Bow Street, or before a Justice of the Peace more immediately situated, which he is to do early in the following Morning, and to take the Addresses of the Witnesses, and warn them to attend with him accordingly.*

Every Patrol when on Nightly Duty, is to wear the Uniform of the Establishment, to have his Appointments with him, his Pistol loaded, and his Sabre worn on the outside of his Coat. He is not to go off the High Road, or into any Public *(or other)* House, *during the time of his Duty (excepting in pursuit of an Offender). He is to make himself known to all Persons in* Carriages, and on Horseback, *by calling out to them as they pass, in a loud and distinct tone of voice, 'Bow Street Patrol'; and should any Patrol be discovered to be* drunk, or intoxicated *when on Duty, he will be forthwith* discharged *from his Situation.*

No Patrol while on Duty, is to deliver his Horse to the care of any other Person, or suffer it to be out of his sight, for the purpose of being put into a Stable, or otherwise.

If any Patrol shall be taken ill, or his Horse become lame, or unfit for duty, he is to report it immediately to Mr DAY, or one of the Inspectors, or Deputy Inspectors; and in case of his Horse being unfit for Duty, he is to patrol on foot (taking his Truncheon, Handcuffs and Pistol with him) and to go not less than half the distance that he would on Horseback.

If any Patrol shall not be met by the other patrol on the Road, in the manner directed, he is to report the same the following morning to Mr DAY, or one of the Inspectors, or Deputy Inspectors; and not any excuse will be admitted for neglecting to make such a Report.

No Patrol is to use his Horse for any other purpose but his regular Duty, nor to keep it at Grass without leave to that effect, nor is he (excepting in the case of illness) to intrust his Horse to the care of any other Person.

No Patrol will be permitted to have any other Occupation, nor to employ himself in any manner which may prevent him from attending immediately *when called upon, to any Duty which the Public Service may require of him whether by day or by night.*

Every Patrol is to reside with his Family *in the House provided at which he is stationed, and which with the Premises attached thereto, is to be kept in a clean and decent condition; he is not to have Pigs, Fowls nor other Animals which feed on Corn; and he is not to be absent more than Two Miles from his Station (excepting on Duty) without leave for that purpose.*

Every Patrol is to attend to his Horse and other Stable Duties, according to the Directions hung up in the Stable.

Whenever the Patrol are ordered to attend an Inspection, they are to appear in the full Uniform of the Establishment, with their Arms and other Appointments which, with their Horses, are to be in perfect order and fit for Service.

If any Patrol shall lose any of his Appointments, they will be replaced at his Expense.

Every Patrol, when from Home is to appear in his Uniform; any omission of this Order will be deemed as shewing that he is ashamed of the Situation which he holds, and consequently unfit to be retained therein.

If it shall appear that any Patrol has by unjust or disreputable Conduct, disgraced the Situation he holds, by obtaining a Bad Character in the neighbourhood in which he is stationed, he will forthwith be dismissed from the Service.

These men, the Bow Street patrols, were still on that same wage, a guinea a week, or three shillings a day, but they do seem to have been provided with accommodation. Mr Day was the Clerk to the Horse Patrol, who later became an Inspector.

In office for the second time, the Home Secretary Sir Robert Peel did excellent work in reforming the criminal law, which was even more complicated, corrupted and unwieldy than the policing of it. For example, there were over 50 separate Acts detailing offences against the person, and 30 or so connected with forgeries. Peel consolidated these into one statute each, and turned his attention to enforcement.

In 1828, he initiated an inquiry into the policing of all London, despite the objections, and made it plain that he thought highly of the work being done by foot and horse patrols out of Bow Street and the other public offices. He wanted a single, united body of men, disciplined and professional, working together across the capital – defined as that area within a 10-mile radius of St Paul's Cathedral, excluding the City of London – responsible to the Home Secretary and funded by taxes. That he actually managed to create such a thing, against powerful and widespread objections that seem incredible now, says a great deal about the mettle of the man.

He called them his 'vigorous preventive police', and their chief target was to be those most visible of crimes: vice, theft, violence, disorder. They were to win the battle of the streets, making London a safe, orderly, pleasant place in which law-abiding citizens could go about their business without fear.

Peel appointed two Commissioners to do the legwork for him, on salaries of £800 per annum, and the three met together for the first time on 6 July 1829. The Commissioners were an Irish barrister, Richard Mayne, and an Irish army officer, Colonel Charles Rowan, lately commanding officer of the 52nd (Oxfordshire) Foot and wounded at Waterloo.

Mayne was the more intelligent of the two, a good communicator and full of ideas, while Rowan was the organiser, the believer in military discipline and an excellent man-manager. Later, when Mayne – then Sir Richard – became sole commissioner, his lack of Rowan's special talents would become apparent.

At their meeting with Peel, Rowan was given the job of raising and organising the new force, which was to have an establishment of 895 constables, 88 sergeants, 20 inspectors and eight superintendents. The Bow Street Horse Patrol, foot patrols and the recently established River Police were to be left on their own for the moment. They would be absorbed into the Metropolitan Police in 1836.

By 29 September, the first day at work for the Metropolitan Police, Rowan had recruited almost that number, in five divisions. By May of the following year, there were 17 operational divisions.

Mayne wrote down his idea of the objectives of the Force, based on Peel's philosophy: 'The primary object of an efficient police is the prevention of crime: the next that of detection and punishment of offenders if crime is committed. To these ends all the efforts of police must be directed. The protection of life and property, the preservation of public tranquillity, and the absence of crime, will alone prove whether those efforts have been successful and whether the objects for which the police were appointed have been attained.'

Rowan expected that regular patrolling, the policeman on the beat, would realise these objectives. In fact, when the first of the new police officers went out on patrol, they were the ones who had to look out for themselves: some were physically attacked, and all were subject to public hostility and criticism, reinforced and amplified by the newspapers. At least one newspaper, however, preached rational moderation. Here is part of an editorial from *The Times*, 25 September 1829:

> *The new police force is on the eve of being brought into action, and of putting to an immediate test the justice of those complaints which have been made by all classes of individuals for more than two centuries, against the total inefficiency of our 'ancient and most reverend watchmen'.*
>
> *The principle on which English Police (as it is called) has hitherto invariably proceeded, is congenial to our national prejudices, leaving men's free agency in a great measure uninterrupted, until it ripens into the actual perpetration of crime. This respect and deference for the freedom of the subject, has nevertheless overshot one purpose, while it served a worse: it has forgotten to protect the innocent, and has transferred all its real benefits to the wrong-doer. The instructions to the new police set out with a formal abandonment of the rule that it should be the sole aim of justice to punish guilt. The theory taught by the new regulations, is that the power to act under them ought to have for its main object the* prevention of crime, *not the execution of the criminal.*

It is true that the forthcoming system may be productive of considerable, though partial evil, if the abuse of such a right and practice as that of interference before the fact be not guarded against with great vigilance and discretion. But if the right be in general exercised on fair grounds of apprehended crime, and from a bona fide *zeal on behalf of the public safety, we do not see that, as a whole, any rational objection can be made to it.*

The Times leader goes on to say that the new officers must be of 'a much more enlarged degree of attainment and intelligence' than we were used to in the watchmen, and that the constables' extensive powers must be exercised with mildness and forbearance. One radical departure in the structure of the Force, in a society used to position and rank being purchased, and/or filled by gentlemen of the higher social classes, was the open promise that any of the lowest ranks could reasonably hope for promotion by merit to the highest:

The pay of the lowest rank is very moderate, being only 3s. per day; and that small salary liable to specific deductions. The inspectors, however, are said to have £100 per annum, and the superintendents £200.

The strength of the metropolitan police as at present constituted, is as follows:- 5 divisions, or companies, each consisting of 1 superintendent, 4 inspectors, 16 serjeants, 144 police constables.

So, for that part of London then designated as comprising 'Mr Peel's project', there were 825 officers and men, about 80 per cent of the original plan, which, considering the time he had, was an outstanding achievement by Charles Rowan.

'If the system be not jobbed,' said *The Times*, by which was meant not turned to private advantage, 'it is one which promises advantageously for the public safety.'

From *The Times*, 7 October 1829, only a few days after the introduction of the Metropolitan Police:

We have several letters by us on the subject of the new police. The advantages of the institution, we think, are already very observable: there is less violence, confusion and open profligacy in the street in which the new police officers are stationed. In one particular an alteration may be made, and will be found necessary: the wages of the new officers are too low. [A watchman said] the new police drove all the bad characters into the city: they fly to the city because they are safer there.

Same paper, same day:

A new Station-house for the metropolitan police was opened yesterday in Great Scotland-yard, opposite the Marshalsea Court, Whitehall. The Commissioners of the new police have given directions that the police constables should, for the future, not bring such frivolous charges to the stations as they did last week, but be more circumspect in their conduct, and apprehend only those persons whom there is an absolute necessity for confining the whole night.

Over the next 20 or so years, the hostility to the new police died away as citizens and officers alike became accustomed to one another, and the notion of policing by consent took over from 'vigorous preventive' action. They carried truncheons but not the firearms of the Army, and were seen in a more friendly, helpful role by those who kept the law.

The success of Sir Robert's 'peelers', or 'bobbies', in greatly reducing crime and producing evidence for convictions silenced the opposers and was copied in other towns, although it was not until 1856 that similar forces were made compulsory throughout England and Wales.

The Horse Patrol formed the embryonic Mounted Branch and was absorbed into the Metropolitan Police in 1836. At its peak, the Branch was over 200 strong. Other police forces, and there were many more then, when every town had its own force, adopted the mounted idea – Newcastle-upon-Tyne, for example, set up a Mounted patrol in 1836.

In modern times, some see the mounted officer as an anachronism, an outdated throwback to an era long gone, but this is by no means a new phenomenon. As the railways spread across the country, highwaymen were forced to seek other employment and the need disappeared for Mounted Police 'to afford Protection to Persons travelling on the High Roads', but a different need soon became apparent. There was poverty and unrest in country areas (easily reached on horseback from central London in those days), leading to cattle and sheep rustling and other thefts of livestock. The Mounted Branch's business in this type of crime, which in some ways was even more dangerous than catching highwaymen, also disappeared as London sprawled ever outwards, and rural villages became suburbs.

Another duty, as message carriers around the Met area, also became redundant when the police embraced the new technology of the telegraph. Meanwhile, one of the main responsibilities of the modern Mounted Branch was growing, as social disorder increased. Previously governments had used the Army to quell riots and civil uprisings, sometimes with dreadful consequences, and Mounted Police proved a better option all round.

With his family, a wee laddie called John Macdonald emigrated from Scotland to Canada in 1820. He grew up to be a lawyer, went into politics and became the first Prime Minister of the new Dominion of Canada in 1867. By 1869 he had agreed terms with the Hudson's Bay Company for the purchase of the huge expanse of the North-West Territories, called Rupert's Land, and set about organising a system of law and order for this wild, inaccessible region of half a million square miles, some of it beyond the Arctic Circle.

Macdonald asked the Army to make a survey, which suggested that a force of 100 or 150 mounted, armed men could do the job. Thus was born the North-West Mounted Rifles, renamed the North-West Mounted Police in 1873, which grew to a force of more than 1,000 men, merged with the Dominion Police in 1920 and was again renamed as the Royal Canadian Mounted Police.

Pictures of Mounties, in their red jackets and Stetson hats, illustrated official Canadian government publications and tourist brochures of the 1880s, and the strong but quiet, heroic and kindly, far-ranging, lonely figure of justice soon caught the imagination of writers who produced novels, Hollywood movies, stage musicals such as *Rose-Marie* (1924) and TV series to capitalise on the romantic image.

'The Mountie always gets his man,' says the legend, a phrase that almost certainly derives from a Montana newspaper, the *Fort Benton Record*, in which the line, 'They fetch their man every time' was used in a report of an arrest of a whisky smuggler in 1877.

The main role of the Mounties in modern Canada is somewhat similar to that of the FBI in the US, a federal law-enforcement agency that, alas, no longer needs horses. The Mounties have dismounted, but police in the larger cities of Canada maintain their own units, with Toronto's the biggest at around 30 horses and 40 officers.

One list of duties for London's Mounted Police given for 1910 included patrolling common lands, controlling strike-breaking violence, escorting members of the monarchy, and searching for lost children and escaped criminals. The modern Metropolitan Police Mounted Branch was really established in 1919, when Lieutenant-Colonel Percy Laurie, retired commanding officer of the Royal Scots Greys cavalry regiment, took up the appointment of Assistant Commissioner 'A' Department. Training in those days was short: officers had three weeks at the reserve stables in Adam and Eve Mews, Kensington, and another similar period at Rochester Row before going out on duty.

Colonel Laurie wanted rather more from his mounted men than such training could possibly provide, and so had land obtained for a new purpose-built riding school at Imber Court, Thames Ditton in Surrey. This was literally a green field site and so Laurie's ideas, based on his Army experience, plus his consultations with many experts in the horse world, produced a facility that was, at the time, the very ideal, and still meets every need asked of it.

One of the great successes of the Metropolitan Police happened soon after Laurie implemented his reforms over 90 years ago, and is still 'remembered' by millions of people who were not there, and was – at least in folklore – all due to one horse.

The new Empire Stadium at Wembley had just been completed, with a capacity of 127,000. Football crowds were generally bigger in those days, with almost everyone standing, but the numbers wanting to see the first Wembley match, the FA Cup Final between Bolton Wanderers and West Ham United, took the authorities by surprise. No one had even thought it worth issuing tickets.

As kick-off time approached on 28 April 1923, there were roughly 100,000 spectators inside the ground and another 100,000 would-be spectators outside. The ones outside charged the gates, burst through and flooded onto the pitch. It was – or appeared to be – an impossible situation. The huge crowd was in a good mood, which could easily have changed. King George V was up there in the Royal Box; there was nothing he could do but his presence may have helped to keep things calm. The problem was: how could the football be played?

Four years earlier, when that eminent Army officer, Colonel Percy Laurie (later Major-General Sir Percy, KCVO, CBE, DSO), had been appointed with his special brief to reorganise the Mounted Branch, he brought with him his own cavalry horse, Quicksilver. He also brought with him, over the next few months, some of the men who had served with him during the Great War in the Royal Scots Greys. There was plenty of precedent for this. At least one Met Police mounted officer, Benjamin Beeson, had been a survivor of the Charge of the Light Brigade.

One of Laurie's First World War veterans was Trooper George Albert Scorey who, through Laurie's influence, managed to duck under the police measuring stick, he being rather less than the 5 feet 9 inches required. In June 1920, after a few months in the Mounted Branch, he formed what was to become a famous partnership with Billy, a seven-year-old grey, officially Horse Number 62.

At the 1923 match there were, in round numbers, 600 officers of whom 400 were in and around the ground, 200 being in reserve, including PC Scorey and Billy. The reserves were called in and Scorey, with fewer than a dozen mounted colleagues and considerable numbers on foot, managed to push the spectators back beyond the playing area. Cinema newsreels and press photographs were all monochrome, and Scorey's grey horse stood out in every picture as shining white.

The Monday papers had a great time of it. Reliable as ever, the *Daily Express* said that a 'handful of mounted police' had cleared the crowds off the pitch led 'by a lion-hearted inspector on a snow-white prancing horse'. Meanwhile, the *Daily Mirror* said that one officer on a white charger won the admiration of everyone there and had been cheered for his work.

Within a few days, Scorey had been publicly identified as the hero, mentioned in the House, and offered many opportunities of celebrity. Not being that sort of a fellow, he returned to his normal duties, partnering Billy until 1930, when the horse died. Percy Laurie had a hoof made into a silver-mounted inkwell, presented it to Scorey, and it came back to the Imber Court museum after Scorey's death in 1965.

The match was ever – and will for ever – be known as 'the white horse final'. A good pub quiz question might be 'Who won it?' (Bolton, 2-0).

In 1929, the centenary of the Metropolitan Police was celebrated with a parade in Hyde Park, including the Mounted Branch of course, and inspection by HRH the Prince of Wales.

During the Second World War, the founder of the People's Dispensary for Sick Animals, Maria Dickin CBE, became aware of the bravery displayed by animals on active service and at the Home Front. Inspired by the animals' devotion to man and duty, Mrs Dickin introduced a medal specifically for animals in war.

The PDSA Dickin Medal, recognised as the animals' Victoria Cross, is awarded to animals displaying conspicuous gallantry or devotion to duty while serving in, or associated with, any branch of the Armed Forces or Civil Defence Units. The PDSA Dickin Medal is the highest accolade any animal can receive while involved in military conflict.

Only three horses have received the PDSA Dickin Medal. All three were Metropolitan Police horses on duty in London during the Second World War.

Citation, police horse Olga: 'While on duty in Tooting, a flying bomb demolished four houses and a plate-glass window crashed immediately in front of her. Olga, after bolting for 100 yards, returned to the scene of the incident and remained on duty with her rider, controlling traffic and assisting rescue organisations.'

Olga was a bay mare, with a narrow white coronet marking, generally being used in crowd control and rescue. It was 3 July 1944, when the V1 buzz bomb was still a novelty, and Olga and PC J E Thwaites, not her usual rider, were patrolling Besley Street, SW16. A V1 fell near the railway line, exploding not far in front of them, blowing up the houses and sending glass everywhere, including a shop window. Four people were killed. Olga, naturally enough, took fright and ran from the scene but PC Thwaites calmed her and brought her back to the scene of her distress, where they could keep sightseers away and Thwaites could assist the survivors.

Citation, police horse Upstart: 'While on duty in Bethnal Green, a flying bomb exploded within 75 yards, showering both horse and rider with broken glass and debris. Upstart was completely unperturbed and remained quietly on duty with his rider controlling traffic etc, until the incident had been dealt with.'

Upstart was a chestnut gelding with four white feet, a small star and a snip (white mark on nose) on his face. He had been at Hyde Park station until an enemy attack on a nearby anti-aircraft post damaged the stables, when he was relocated to east London. Still in 1944 and at the height of the V1 campaign, when these self-propelled bombs could land anywhere, one narrowly missed a police horse and its rider, Divisional Inspector J Morley, but both remained calm enough to keep traffic and people moving.

Citation, police horse Regal: 'Was twice in burning stables caused by explosive incendiaries at Muswell Hill. Although receiving minor injuries, being covered by debris and close to the flames, this horse showed no signs of panic.'

Regal was a bay gelding with a small white star on his forehead and white socks on his hind legs. His handler was PC Hector Poole. In 1941, as the London Blitz was slowing down, incendiary bombs fell on the Muswell Hill station, starting a fire in the forage room that soon spread to the stalls, where Regal was. Despite all the flames and smoke, he allowed himself to be led quietly away. Three years later, during the V1 campaign, a buzz bomb fell beside the police station. The roof partially collapsed and debris hit and injured Regal. Once more, he made no fuss.

Post-war, when no one questioned the need for Mounted Police, there were many major incidents in which they figured prominently. One example was the 1976 riot at Notting Hill Carnival, 10 years after its inception, when 150,000 people came, groups of young men got into fights, and more than 400 officers and civilian staff were injured.

One day in July 1982, Tuesday the 20th, changed things for ever. This is how *Time Magazine* saw it:

> *The bright morning sun sparkled off the plumed metal helmets of the Blues and Royals troopers of the Queen's Household Cavalry as they left their barracks for the daily mounting of the guard at Whitehall. Resplendent in blue tunics, white buckskin breeches and silver-colored breastplates, the tips of their unsheathed swords jauntily resting on their right shoulders, the colorful 16-man troop trotted along Hyde Park's South Carriage Drive while admiring tourists lolled in the grass and snapped pictures. The cavalrymen never reached their destination.*

At 10:43 a large nail bomb, hidden in a blue Austin car parked on South Carriage Drive, exploded (see also page 15).

The thought that something similar could happen today much exercises minds in the Mounted Branch and is embedded in training from the early days at Imber Court.

In attaining all of the objectives of Mounted Police – which, as ACC Rod Hansen says, range from 'Polo mints in the playground to routine policing, to front-line commitments in full body armour, to counter-terrorism, to crowd management' – much depends on the approval and co-operation of the public, in a country which believes in policing by consent. The degree of esteem and respect in which the police are held is hugely important, and surely the Mounted Police are a vital factor in keeping that esteem and respect as high as possible.

Special thanks are due to PC Phil Cole for his help with this history.

Horses have been used by police in Victoria since the Military Mounted Police rode into the colony in 1836. The establishment of Victoria Police brought several Mounted Units together as the Mounted Branch. As the state flourished, horse and rider numbers increased, as did the scale of crime. Mounted Police hunted the Ned Kelly gang across the state, with three officers killed, until the final shoot-out at Glenrowan in 1880.

At the start of the twentieth century, there were 211 Mounted-Police stations in Victoria. Soon, as elsewhere, the motorcar was seen as a superior replacement for the horse (not forgetting that previous 'patrol cars' had been pulled by horses) and the number of Mounted stations declined rapidly, although the last of the out-stations would not close until 1965. That was at Buninyong, once the first inland town of Victoria and the starting point of the 1850s gold rush, but now a suburb of Ballarat.

Today, the Melbourne stables are the original ones, built in 1912 close to St Kilda Road in Southbank, and they can take 50 horses. Crowd-control high points include the F1

Grand Prix, the Motorcycle Grand Prix, New Year's Eve celebrations and parades such as Anzac Day.

Horses are warmblood types, specially bred for police work at the Mounted Branch, and must be at least 16.2 hands. Members of Victoria Police can apply to work at the Mounted Branch after they have completed at least two years' service. Applicants must be able to ride before they apply for a position at the Branch.